Mirror of the Century

THE STRAND MAGAZINE 1891-1950

BOOKS BY REGINALD POUND

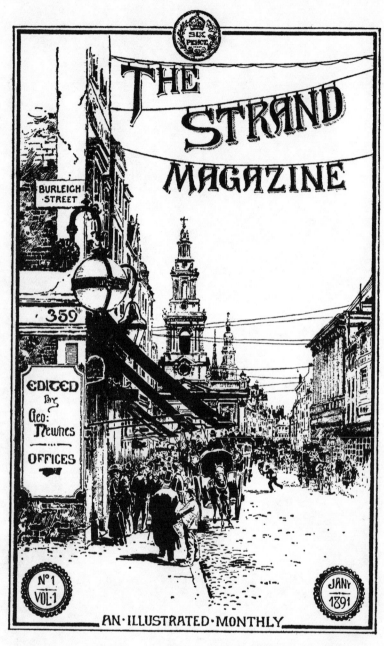

SIX PENCE

THE STRAND MAGAZINE

BURLEIGH STREET

359

EDITED by Geo: Newnes

OFFICES

Nº 1
VOL·1

JANY
1891

AN·ILLUSTRATED·MONTHLY

Cover drawing, from the original by G. H. Haite, familiar to two
generations of readers in every part of the English-speaking world.

Mirror of the Century

THE STRAND MAGAZINE 1891–1950

REGINALD POUND

South Brunswick
New York: A. S. Barnes and Co.

© Reginald Pound, 1966

Library of Congress Catalogue Card Number: 67-12836

A. S. Barnes and Co., Inc.

Cranbury, New Jersey

6587

Printed in the United States of America

CONTENTS

ILLUSTRATIONS

AUTHOR'S ACKNOWLEDGMENTS

As the author of a number of biographical and other works, I am aware of the invidiousness of listing the names of those who have responded, often most generously, to requests for information, advice, and other help. It is an inadequate form of appreciation, which some critics have suggested should be confined to the private domain. With that churlish view I find it impossible to agree.

I deem it a courtesy, if not a duty, to record my grateful thanks to the following friends, acquaintances, former colleagues, and correspondents, who have assisted the labours that have resulted in this book:

Mr James Hillyard and Mr Sydney Hillyard, nephews of the late Sir George Newnes, and Mrs Neville Foster and Mrs A. Dillon-Clarke, his nieces; Mr Herbert Tingay, formerly chairman of Messrs George Newnes, Limited; Mr Augustus Baker and the late E. N. Sanders, both for many years members of *The Strand Magazine* editorial staff; Miss Winifred Paget (daughter of the late Sidney Paget, illustrator of the Sherlock Holmes stories); Mr. Frank R. Singleton, Librarian, The *Guardian*; Professor J. O. Baylen, of Mississippi State University (an authority on W. T. Stead); the Rev. R. Mansfield, M.A., Ph.D., and Miss Ethel Gold, for information concerning the Rev. T. M. Newnes; Sir Alfred Watson; Mr Frank Spencer, Headmaster, Silcoates School, and his predecessor, the late Sydney H. Moore, M.A.; the Secretary of the Congregational Union of England and Wales; Mr T. G. Davies; Mrs G. Claydon; the Secretary, City of London School, and the Honorary Editor, City of London School *Register*; the City Librarian, Birmingham; Messrs Emmott & Co. Ltd.; Messrs Taylor, Garnett, Evans & Co. Ltd.;

the late Miss Naomi Royde-Smith (Mrs Ernest Milton);
Mr Leonard Crocombe; Lady Newnes; Lord Rothermere;
Sir Geoffrey Harmsworth, Bart; the late Sir Grimwood
Mears; Mr Henry Williamson; Mr Duncan Lush; the
Publicity Department, Messrs W. H. Smith & Son, Ltd.; the
Publicity Department, B.B.C.; Mr Charles Bovill; Mr
Andrew Dakers; Mr R. P. Cole, Secretary, Messrs George
Newnes, Ltd.; Mr E. V. Merrett, Librarian, London Express
Newspapers, Ltd.; Mr Percy V. Bradshaw; Mr Macdonald
Hastings; Mr Alan Wykes; Mr David Arkell; the Secretary
of the Society for Psychical Research (concerning Sir A.
Conan Doyle); Mr Alex McKay, managing director, Messrs
George Newnes, Ltd.; Mr Charles Morris; and Mr M. F.
Holder, manager of Newnes Press Service, and his staff.

Extracts from Chapters 1 and 5 were serialised in *The
Times*, January 13 and 14, 1966.

39 Welbeck Street, W.1.   R.P.

ONE

A British Institution

'Mr Churchill to speak to you.' It seemed unlikely that the leader of the nation who had so recently had direct telephonic access to the White House and the Kremlin now desired to be connected personally with the office of *The Strand Magazine* at Tower House, Southampton Street, London, W.C.2. The switchboard operator was asked to check back. She reported: 'Yes, Mr Churchill would be glad to talk to you about his paintings.'

It was 1945. He had just suffered the great reverse of his political career, his rejection by the British people at the general election that July. (He was possibly mistaken in seeing it as an affront to himself rather than to his party.) Like *The Strand Magazine*, shorn of its former glory by paper rationing and a falling market, he was cut down in size. Bereft of power, he may have had visions of the wilderness again, of the years of humbling frustration between the wars when even some of his intimates doubted his future. 'Churchill?' Lord Beaverbrook said sharply when, some time in 1932, *Daily Express* editorial matters were being discussed at his place near Leatherhead and I proposed Churchill as a political contributor. 'Why Churchill? He's a busted flush.'

As balm in what for him were difficult as well as disappointing times, Churchill had gone back to the painting in oils that he first practised in 1915 when, after another abrupt break in his public life as First Lord of the Admiralty, he felt, as he afterwards put it, 'like a sea-beast fished up from the depths, or a diver too suddenly hoisted'.

He reminded me, talking on the telephone from Chartwell,

that he had written with enthusiasm about his hobby in two articles entitled *Painting as a Pastime* that appeared in *The Strand Magazine* in December 1921 and January 1922. The first was illustrated by reproductions of his paintings in colour, the second in half-tone, then still the dominant process in picture reproduction. He was paid £500 for the text and £400 for the use of the pictures accompanying it. Introducing himself to the readers as an amateur painter, he wrote: 'There is no subject on which I feel more humble and at the same time more natural. I know of nothing which, without exhausting the body, more entirely absorbs the mind.' He was careful to explain that he did not 'submit these sketches to the public gaze because I am under any illusion about their merit'. The disavowal, as I discovered for myself, hid no private conceit. When, a little later on, I suggested to him that he should allow his work to be put on show in a public gallery for the benefit of the Artists' Benevolent Fund he would not hear of it.

The purpose of his telephone call was to discover which of his latest works I would 'care to consider' reproducing in full colour, in which process he understood there had been many improvements during the intervening twenty-five years. The surmise was correct. Colour printing, in which George Newnes, Limited, publishers of *The Strand Magazine*, promoted some of the most successful developments, had attained standards of fidelity in reproduction far beyond those of 1921.

What I wondered as he spoke was: Did he realise the limits imposed by our reduced page-size, due to the rigid paper control of the war years? It was a declension that put *The Strand* in the new 'pocket' class of magazine. Was it likely that he had seen a copy during his tumultuous preoccupations of the last half decade? 'Of course, I know your difficulties', he said, anticipating my doubt and removing it. The matter of payment was touched on. He inquired, not in vain: 'Would a thousand pounds be reasonable?' He was coming up to town that week. 'Pray, would it be convenient to you to call and see me at noon on Friday?'

2

There were two hour-long sessions at his bedside in the small room at the top of 28 Hyde Park Gate. He expressed his pleasure at renewing his old standing with the magazine, despite its diminished prestige. 'You know, I have a long and happy association with *The Strand*. Is there any hope of your restoring its size? It used to look so very prosperous.' He spoke of his journalism. 'After all, I *am* a member of your profession. I've never had any money except what my pen has brought me.' He thought for a moment and added, as if scrupulous about accuracy: 'I did once have a modest fortune. It was a *very* modest one' (deriving, one understood, from an Irish property left him by a distant relative).

His impulse to write may have been spurred by example as well as by necessity. His father, Lord Randolph, was paid 2,000 guineas for 20 articles on South Africa. In 1895, young Winston contracted with the London *Daily Telegraph* to send articles from the North-West Frontier at the rate of £5 a column. He was paid £250 a month by the *Morning Post* as that newspaper's correspondent with the Forces in the South African war. Before he was 30, he saved £4,500 of his earnings from articles, books and lectures.

He was a journalist without the journalist's gregariousness. He was seldom seen in Fleet Street, though he was known personally to many of its editors and reporters. In the early years one of his closest friends there was Alfred Harmsworth, who assured him publicity rather than income. It was not until thirty years later, in his wilderness term, that he wrote regularly for the Harmsworth newspapers. He was then engaged to write a weekly article for the *Daily Mail*: fee per article, £180. It may have been an essential item of his finances at the time. It fell to me, as the literary editor of the *Daily Mail*, to discuss with him on the telephone the subjects he was to write about. His voice comes to me now from afar. 'Do you mind if I attack Sir John Simon?' Or: 'I would like to have a go at those dirty little Nazis.' His humour and courtesy made those exchanges more than a professional pleasure. I recall his dependability as a contributor. His copy always arrived 'clean' and on the appointed day.

His long connection with *The Strand Magazine* was assumed to have begun with the publication in 1908 of a series of nine articles, *My African Journey*, describing his travels in Kenya, Uganda and neighbouring territories. He received £150 per article and £30 for the photographs which were supplied as illustrations; more than Kipling, whom *The Strand* was paying £90 for his short stories; more than W. W. Jacobs, whose rate at that time was £110 for a story.

Who, then, was the Winston Spencer who wrote the article headed *The Most Sensational Motor Ride* in *The Strand* for December 1901? It told of a circus act that was thrilling American audiences, its hero a one-legged man who drove a primitive motorcar down a ramp as steep as a ski-jump at breakneck speed. It was a kind of feat that would have stirred Churchill's imagination: ' . . . as an exemplification of iron nerves, cool judgment and levelheadedness, the achievement would be difficult to excel'. He had recently been on a lecture tour in the U.S. He was also in correspondence with the American novelist, Winston Churchill, about the awkward similarity of their names. He told the American Churchill that to avoid clashing he would in future sign his press contributions by the name of Winston Spencer Churchill (a differentiation that he was able to drop as soon as he became an M.P.).

Did he briefly experiment with the pseudonym of Winston Spencer? Unfortunately, *The Strand Magazine* account books do not enlighten us. Payment for the article was made to someone named F. A. Talbot. For the other Winston Churchill good came out of the confusion. The American *Bookman* recorded in 1901 that his best-selling novel, *The Crisis*, 'at first sold chiefly because it was imagined that the author was Mr Winston Spencer Churchill'.

3

Here he was, forty years on, telling me: 'I've just had an offer from an American magazine, *Collier's*. If I accept it, I shall be able to say that I am one of the world's highest paid writers.' He was in bed. He spoke along his cigar, from which there dangled a ribbon of soggy leaf. 'I've signed nothing yet,' he said, and grinned his satisfaction at still being wanted by the world. He no longer had the £10,000 a year of a Prime Minister. Presumably, literary earnings were important again.

His cousin, Clare Sheridan, the sculptor, wrote that 'he never knew want', implying, it seemed from her tone, some lack of sympathy with those who did. From what he wrote about Balfour in *Great Contemporaries* it could be inferred that he was by no means insensitive to the harassments of ordinary existence: 'He was never seriously worried about money; he never had to face the problem of earning his livelihood, or of paying the bills for the common necessities of life.'

That there were times when apparently he needed money as urgently as any of the less well-placed freelances of the profession (who should have elected him their patron saint), I gathered from a previous occupant of *The Strand* editorial chair, Reeves Shaw, who told me that he had more than once had cheques drawn at Churchill's urgent request and sent to him by hand. In the correspondence files there were letters from Churchill courteously asking for payment, 'if possible, by Monday morning'. At the *Daily Mail* in the '30s it was authoritatively confided that he was a recipient of the private bounty of the chief proprietor, the first Lord Rothermere.

His income from journalism in those days was none the less considerable, if intermittent. *The Strand Magazine* bought his articles at £450 each. He was selling quantities of material direct to American and overseas newspapers. 'I earned my living by dictating articles,' he wrote, looking back over the inter-war years, and declared: 'With my happy family around me, I dwelt at peace within my habitation.'

Arising out of those bedside talks, two sets of Churchill's paintings appeared in *The Strand Magazine* for July and August 1946. Among the thirty originals from which I made the final choice (while in the office they were insured for £100 each) were a study of elephants in the circus ring, soldiers of the First World War with their womenfolk at Victoria Station, and a pack of foxhounds moving under trees in early morning light. He shook his head gravely when I begged his permission to use them. I pleaded. He shook his head again. I said that readers would be delighted by his choice and rendering of those subjects. Of the elephants I wrote in my diary: 'Their ungainliness and his inexperience blend into a peculiarly touching cartoon.' I suppose my disappointment was obvious. 'They're from photographs. It wouldn't be fair to pass them off as my original work. Would it?' There was no more to be said.

A number of people, hearing that the pictures were in our temporary keeping, asked permission to see them. The popular cartoonist of the *Daily Express*, Strube, was one of the callers. He was taken by surprise at the virtuosity of a statesman whose career he had caricatured for more than thirty years. Another of the visitors was Tommy Handley, then one of the nation's idols as the comedian of the B.B.C. programme called ITMA. He was another passionately uncritical admirer of Churchill's work.

The pictures, displaying a versatility and command that astonished many, made a brave, exhilarating show in those attenuated pages of *The Strand* that summer. I remember a phrase from one of the numerous letters of appreciation received in the office: 'As good as a one-man Royal Academy!' That Churchill could not draw was of no consequence. He complained to me: 'I can't draw hands.' I said: 'You can draw trees and that's quite a test.' He was not appeased. 'I can't draw hands,' he repeated with regret in his voice. He mentioned that he had been given painting lessons by Sir John Lavery, Walter Sickert, Sir William Nicholson, and Sir Oswald Birley. Lady Lavery had told me that at one period he 'haunted John's studio'. She remembered that once, while her husband was at work on a portrait, Churchill, who had been looking on, murmured to her: 'It makes me feel very humble. I've a lot to learn.' He said to me during our bedroom interview: 'You see that picture in the alcove?' I went and stood before it, a study of a small chateau. 'It was sent anonymously to an exhibition and gained first place.' His eyes reflected his pleasure in recalling that little triumph.

Naming his artist friends impelled him to scornful utterance about postwar art trends. 'They're deluding the people!' he exclaimed fiercely. He raised his cigar on high as if it were a dagger to be plunged into a hated enemy.

He referred again to the articles on painting that he had written for *The Strand* 'all those years ago'. It gratified him to recall that they were the main substance of a book that sold well. Many who read it, he said, wrote to thank him 'for sending them off on the same happy voyage of discovery. They found, as I have, that painting is the best possible recreation for the overburdened mind'. It was in the same gentle tone that he offered to autograph for me a large colour proof of one of the pictures we had chosen for the magazine. Having done it, with a massive gold fountain-pen, he asked: 'Would you like me to do another for you?' and signed it as deliberately as if he were putting his name to a treaty.

He explained that he stayed in bed until lunch time because the doctors said that he was tired. 'I suppose they know.' The jacket of his crimson pyjamas was unbuttoned, showing a massive plinth of neck under the promontory jaw. Rising from the chair that he had told me to draw up to the bed, I took my leave of him, ruefully reflecting that both Winston Churchill and *The Strand Magazine* had seen their best days.

4

The 1890s favoured many more adventurous literary experiments than *The Strand Magazine*, which was disregarded, if not despised, by the restless coteries of *The Yellow Book* and *The Savoy*. Certainly the middle-classes of England never cast a clearer image of themselves in print than they did in *The Strand Magazine*. Confirming their preference for mental as well as physical comfort, for more than half a century it faithfully mirrored their tastes, prejudices, and intellectual limitations. From them it drew a large and loyal readership that was the envy of the publishing world.

From the beginning, *The Strand* projected the sense of responsibility that was closely related to the moral temper of its founding years, when 'Mr Editor' was a vastly respected entity, infallibly wise and just, and always in the people's fancy, benignly bearded. That concept, and the probity it implied, undoubtedly accounted for Queen Victoria's approval of the publication in an early issue of the full-page drawing captioned 'The Queen's First Baby: Drawn and Etched by Her Majesty'. Shortly afterwards, there was deferential acknowledgment of her help in preparing a sixteen-page article on the dolls of her infancy. 'Her Majesty, in addition to giving us every facility for obtaining photographs of the dolls, has been graciously pleased to read and revise this article. Her Majesty's corrections are given in the form of footnotes.' Against a reference to 'the celebrated Taglioni and her sisters', the Queen wrote marginally on the proof: 'She had none.' Where it was suggested that she, 'the Princess, must at an early age have been expert with her knitting needles', she noted in her puissant hand: 'No, Baroness Lehzen did the minute work.'

For *The Strand Magazine* that august patronage was as good as the Royal Warrant. Apart from being a source of lively enterprise in the advertising department, it was recognition from on high of the fast expanding power of print and publication, of the rise of 'the Fourth Estate—the Reporters' Gallery yonder'.[1] Fleet Street was emerging from its age of portentous anonymity. The majesty of the three-column leader was being trampled under by the march of the all-conquering paragraph, instrument of a revolution greater than any accomplished by the sword. A more urgent momentum thundered through the machine-rooms of St Bride's and Whitefriars, E.C. The occupational attar of ink and oil and hot metal was being compounded by a new alchemy. The art departments glowed with the livid chemical lights of experiments in speedier picture reproduction. A more complex network of wires festooned the Fleet Street sky, linking Thackeray's 'great engine of the Press' with the uttermost places of the earth. Penetrating the hub of the journalists' universe was a sense of tremendous impending change, of an irresistible force moving forward to kindle and exploit the vivacity of the new century.

[1] Carlyle: *Heroes and Hero-Worship*; see also Macaulay: *Edinburgh Review*, 1828.

Arriving on that propitious scene, partly by accident and perfectly matching its time, *The Strand Magazine* soon attained the status of a national institution. No other magazine in Great Britain ever reached that eminence of popular esteem. *The Strand* radiated 'the wonder of the world', that naive, sincere, bright-morning quality which disarms sophistication and puts cynicism to flight. Responsible and yet *dégagé*, developing its own ethos of dignity and popularity, it became as much a symbol of immutable British order as Bank Holidays and the Changing of the Guard.

'*The Queen's First Baby.*' An etching by Queen Victoria, printed in an early issue of *The Strand Magazine* 'by Her Majesty's Special Permission'.

TWO

Triviality Makes News

I

The Strand Magazine was founded by George Newnes in 1891 on the profits of his remarkably successful weekly paper *Tit-Bits*. As an industry, periodical publishing has always flourished largely by a buccaneering imitation of other people's successes. In that sense, Newnes was an exception, an innovator. The idea of *Tit-Bits*, which quickened life for a vast mass of lower middle-class readers of all ages, came in one of those flashes of astuteness that, especially in his *milieu* and time, were apt to be received as the intuition of genius. Certainly no prototype for *Tit-Bits* existed.

In notes dictated for his autobiography, which was never written, Newnes told how, as a young Manchester business man, he went home one evening and, as was his custom, at supper read out to his wife the news in a local evening paper. A report of a railway mishap, in which the children of the stationmaster at Halstead, near Knockholt, Kent, were trapped in some coaches that ran amok during shunting, had a sudden powerful activating effect on his imagination. 'Why shouldn't there be a paper filled with tit-bits like that?' He produced the answer within the next few weeks, his own paper called *Tit-Bits*.

Research for the present work shows that a news item headed 'A Runaway Train' appeared in the *Manchester Evening News* on Wednesday, August 24, 1881.[1] It was one of a number of short news stories that made up a page, among them a horrific mention of the death from hydrophobia of Eugene Clarkson, Q.C. The layout of the first issue of *Tit-Bits*

---

[1] See facing page 24, where the news item is reproduced for the first time since its original publication in 1881.

suggests that the *Manchester Evening News* supplied more than the inspiration of a solitary news item to the changes that ensued in Fleet Street, the worst excesses of which were to be frequently deplored by that newspaper's senior partner, the *Manchester Guardian* (now the *Guardian*). *Tit-Bits* was undeniably the matrix of twentieth-century popular journalism. The sub-editors of the *Manchester Evening News* should not be deprived of their title to a footnote in the records.

The pervasive force of Newnes's founding publication was clearly as incidental in its origin as the majestic effect of Isaac Newton's falling apple or the no less reverberating impact of James Watts's observation of the steaming kettle. Expressing the common mental banality of broad layers of society, an insignificant news item was seized on by a typically acquisitive mind and transformed into the touchstone of change. It was not a revolution, though commonly so called, for revolution implies shock. Prodigious innovation is a more accurate appraisal of the developments initiated by Newnes and carried forward and spread wider by his predatory rivals. And far from having run its course these eighty years after, it is gaining new momentum in countries where illiteracy is a greater problem than it was with us when Newnes, in conjunction with the 1870 Education Act, assailed it with his journalism of the paragraph.

2

There were social critics who believed that the kind of journalism to which Newnes opened the floodgates in 1881 perverted the aims of the 1870 Education Act and the supplementary legislation that came after. The publication in 1959 of the definitive biography of Lord Northcliffe (Alfred Harmsworth) reinforced the view that the 'new' journalism broadcast information at the expense of knowledge and encouraged the Philistinism which Matthew Arnold, obsessively concerned for the cultural health of the nation, feared so much.

What has never been clarified is the formula by which that effect was to be countered in the face of an unprecedented population rise, an accelerating telegraphic system created by the General Post Office, the extension of roads, railways and transport in general, and particularly by the abolition of the paper duties. Cheaper paper yielded results that, as Gladstone said in a prophetic moment, 'will not be fully apparent until we of the nineteenth century are gone'. His statute of repeal encouraged the search for new ways of making paper, culminating in a newsprint industry that has kept the presses of the world in constant motion ever since. Cheaper paper meant more newspapers and more periodicals. They in turn incited the demand for faster printing, which led to the rotary press.

The education idealists, some protesting, some accepting, bowed to the inevitable. Their fears were renewed and confirmed by the technical discoveries that almost overnight displaced handset type and transformed the alphabet into a rampageous invading army that could not be kept out of the most cloistered parts of the social fabric.

It was remarkable that the forces of such momentous change did not derive in the first place from the profession most immediately affected by them. The proprietors, managers, and editors of Fleet Street, traditionally alert to every beat of the public pulse, seem to have been indifferent to the implications of popular education and the multiplicity and variety of the appetites it would create. It is hard to believe that foresight deserted them or that they were influenced, for example, by fears that increased reading would expose the nation to noxious political infections from the Continent.

Yet 'the signs of the times' could hardly have been more obvious. The inspiration of the great Education Act was the need to stimulate more mental skills, compensating for the still relative smallness of the population of England in a world of widening horizons. Apparently no one was willing to invest in the new literacy. It was left to amateur insight and enterprise to exploit the world's first mass reading public.

3

At 30, George Newnes was a bold-chested, short-legged, alert man who had grown a beard as an affectation of seniority rather than as an assertion of masculinity. Endowed with an air of natural authority, he had an eagle glint in his eye suggesting that not for long would he be confined to an environment sufficiently described by his suburban address, Sunnyside, Stretford, Manchester, a semi-detached villa. He was the local representative of a London firm of haberdashers in the service of whose fancy-goods department he drove through the streets of Manchester in a light trap with a smartly harnessed cob.

His father was a Congregational minister, the Rev. Thomas Mold Newnes (1811-1884), of Preston Gubbals, near Shrewsbury. At the time of George's birth, in the year of the Great Exhibition, 1851, Newnes senior was pastor of Glenorchy Chapel, Matlock Bath, Derbyshire. His wife was Sarah Urquhart, from Dundee. It seems that an atavistic spell was put upon her. She was intermittently overwhelmed by a longing for the sea that would not be denied. With a whispered word of warning to her husband, she would suddenly depart from the manse on voyages in coastal trading vessels or the Irish mailboats. Virginia Woolf, in search of the minor apparitions that haunt biography, pictured her standing on a pitching deck, with 'hairy monsters in sou'westers lurching and spitting . . . yet treating the solitary young woman who stands in shawl and poke bonnet gazing, gazing, not without kindness. No, no, no! She will not leave the deck. She will stand there till it is quite dark, thank you!'[1] It was said that her children learnt only later in life that on those mysterious absences she went down to the sea in ships. Coming back, she appears to have been subject to an equally demanding compulsion to 'work for months among the Midland poor'.

Photographs and family anecdotes represented her as being rigidly severe in demeanour. The pastor, given to occasional high spirits with their children, would be checked by a voice bidding him remember the end to which all must come. Every romp was brought to a close with prayer. There was a long surviving memory of the six Newnes children on their knees at the manse, giving thanks after a Christmas party.

'Intended for the ministry', George Newnes was sent to Silcoates, near Wakefield, Yorkshire, a boarding school for the

[1] *London Mercury*, vol. 9.

sons of Congregational ministers and missionaries. Far-off places, such as Chinsura, Madras, Mauritius, Travancore, were entered in the register as addresses of the parents. George Newnes's name first appeared in the records in 1857, when he was six. Looking back, he remembered 'the delicious spit-roasted Sunday joints', and grimaced at his no less vivid recollection of 'the unvarying rice puddings'.

One of his Silcoates contemporaries, W. T. Stead (1849-1912), sometime editor of the *Pall Mall Gazette* and the most celebrated journalist of his day, said that Silcoates was associated with the happiest part of his boyhood and that he learnt there 'three important things—Christianity, cricket, and democracy'. Considering that the average number of pupils was no more than forty, it was remarkable that another Silcoates boy, Edwin Lawrence Godkin, who was there from 1841 to 1845, achieved high journalistic repute as the founder and editor of *The Nation*, the American radical journal which Lord Bryce, British ambassador at Washington, pronounced 'the best weekly in the world'. Those Silcoates successes were proof that the Nonconformist intelligence could not be suppressed or weakened by the interdict that had for so long excluded it from the universities.

George Newnes was at two other schools before going out into the world: a 'boarding academy' called Shireland Hall, Cape Hill, Birmingham, and the City of London School, then in Milk Street, Cheapside, E.C. The *Dictionary of National Biography* states that he was educated at the City of London School. He was there two terms only, spring and summer, 1866. In that brief period he was a contemporary of a future Prime Minister, H. H. Asquith, with whom he competed in a school essay competition. The prize was won by the future founder of one of the twentieth century's foremost publishing houses.

4

The Newneses went to live at 33 Colebrook Row, near the Angel at Islington, one of two terraces of early Victorian houses, some with elegant little balconies, facing each other across a rectangular strip of ground which today provides play space for the young and a bench or two for the old. Much of Colebrook Row still looks as if it belongs to the street directories of a hundred and fifty years ago. From there, George Newnes walked every morning down the long City Road to school.

There was sharp parental disappointment that he showed no desire to follow in his father's dedicated footsteps. When it seemed certain that he was unlikely to experience 'a call', the easy course was chosen of placing him as an apprentice in the City, bringing his formal education abruptly to a close at 16. His father 'went to see some people he knew, haberdashers in a fair way of business', trading under what name, and precisely where, was not recorded. Bound to them for five years, serving most of the time in the basement Entering Room where the sales ledgers were kept, he said that he felt like 'a trapped animal'. Anonymous in the London pavement throng, he 'constantly enjoyed' staring into the windows of the newsagents' shops, 'whiling away happy hours in Camden Passage', then Islington's secondhand book mart.

He would stand on the raised pavement by the Angel and watch the horse traffic arrive in a heaving climax of effort at the end of the long uphill pull from the City, Clerkenwell and Holborn. It confirmed the impression of Islington as a township autonomously detached from the metropolis. The clatter of crinoline hoops had not wholly died away with other echoes of the past, though it may not have been heard on the narrow staircases of Colebrook Row. Not many years before, Charles Lamb had taken the Islington air of a morning and there was still the sight of trees between roofs to remind you of its village origins and that Monday's washing had flapped in jolly gardens where now it hung limp in grimy backyards. Here were the curtained lodging-houses, the steaming tripe shops, the rowdy gin palaces, that Gissing caused Henry Ryecroft to recall as the 'dear old horrors' of his London youth, object lessons for the nineteenth-century social reformers who were insisting so pathetically, as it now appears, that the abolition of poverty would be the end of other evils, including crime.

Newnes made it clear in his scanty personal notes that he

was aware of the far from lofty tone of the publications that provided much of the turnover of the Islington newsagents in those days. Their counters were piled with sensational novelettes at a penny or twopence each. The same dubious tastes were being exploited by a variety of racing sheets which, apart from their ruling passion, gave unabashed currency to smutty stories and made hilarious play with the *double entendre*. Sunday newspapers fed the appetites of those who relished the more lurid dramas of the police courts and the horrors of the hangman's trade. Supply and demand were unconcealed 'The tide of filth' ran so strongly that in 1857 an Obscene Publications Bill was passed.

Like John Cassell, 'the Manchester carpenter', a more experienced reformer who also left his name as the imprint of a London publishing house, George Newnes was ardent in desiring to see a curb put to those excesses of the printed word. Also like Cassell, Newnes profited from his provincial business experience. Cassell originally sold tea and coffee by mail order and through local agents. Newnes sold the fancy-goods of the haberdashery trade, and in doing so gained useful knowledge of the preferences and prejudices of the lower middle classes.

He may have had the vision that sees in trifles the making of great things; more surely, his strongest feeling was for business, subject always to the compulsions of his upbringing. He never carried himself as if he had the favour of the gods. On the contrary, he would have been astounded if he could have moved forward in time from the precipitating moment in the parlour of his little house in a Manchester suburb to find himself the subject of measured assessment in the official history of *The Times*. There it is written: 'He was destined to modify in the most profound degree, the intellectual, social and political tone of the Press as a whole.'

It was he and the most ruthless of his rivals, the Harmsworths, who reaped the harvest of the Education Act of 1870. In *The Long Revolution*,[1] Raymond Williams wrote of 'the myth of 1870' maintaining that there was 'majority literacy before'. Another student of the cultural position at that time,

[1] Chatto & Windus, 1961.

R. K. C. Ensor, insisted that 'the Act of 1870 was a battle with illiteracy'.[1] In that battle, Newnes and the Harmsworths marshalled readers by the million where previously they were to be numbered by the thousand. Another estimate of the effect of Newnes's journalism in relation to the Education Act was made in a survey published three years after his death. '*Tit-Bits* marked the commencement of a new era in the history of the English Press and of the English nation.'[2]

As for his imitators, some benefited enormously. The 'hundred or so' fortunes that Alfred Harmsworth (Northcliffe) computed to be the outcome of his own publishing exploits could be traced back to Newnes's originating impulse. 'Ye gods!' a critic in an exclamatory mood wrote in *The Caxton Magazine* years after. 'If there had been no *Tit-Bits*, it is tolerably certain that there would have been no *Daily Mail*, no *Daily Express*!'

That the logic of those publishing events can be so briskly defined is open to question. The light of the new century was breaking in the sky. Men's minds were invigorated by the prospect. If Newnes had not grasped the opportunity that lay before him, someone equally quick at an inference would have done so. What is certain is that he profited less than his rivals.

[1] *England: 1870-1914* (Oxford, 1936).
[2] *The Influence of the Press* by R. A. Scott James (1913).

THREE

March of the ' Tit-Bits' Brigade

I

Moving busily about his commercial territory between Manchester and Liverpool, George Newnes may have seen the inside of a print shop. He knew nothing of printing or editorial matters. Neither had he the capital to start as a publisher.

He had no luck in his efforts to persuade other business men to venture the few hundreds he needed. There was a frustrating interview with 'a wealthy Manchester business man who walked to and fro in the library of his house in the suburbs'. Newnes was so upset by the curt rejection of his offer of a half-share in his proposed paper for £500 that, walking back to Stretford 'in a mood of deep abstraction', he tripped over a kerb and fell. 'No—no—it's not *that*!' he explained, aware of a policeman's suspicious attention. 'I wasn't looking where I was going.' He had sprained an ankle and was helped into a house nearby, where he was given first-aid by the sympathetic occupants, an old man and his wife.

Offers of the half-share made to Manchester printing firms met with no better response, while his request for credit was also unsuccessful. He and his wife, the daughter of a Leicester Congregational minister named Hillyard, went on snipping out things that interested them in the local and national press. A selection was made up into a 'dummy' of his proposed new weekly. His conviction of the fitness of the title he had chosen for it was so strong that he was afraid to pass newsagents' shops lest he should find that he had been forestalled. It is a familiar neurosis of the periodical publishing trade.

Examination of the first issue of *Tit-Bits* provides proof of the inexperienced hand that saw it to press. There was plenty of unused capacity in the Manchester printing shops. A master printer would have been likely to look on the setting up of such a flimsy production as practice for his apprentices rather than as serious work for his skilled men. *Tit-Bits* No. 1 bears the marks of being hastily jobbed, as if the printer had privately decided that there was no future in it for him.

Newnes had solved his financial difficulty by opening a vegetarian restaurant in the basement of 2 Pall Mall, Manchester, a winding street of narrow pavements that remains a poor compliment to its London namesake. There were already other vegetarian establishments in the city, a symptom perhaps of 'the strain of modern life', the theme of much contemporary philosophising, and a euphemism for the social neurasthenia that was to deepen into our age of anxiety. The bland assurances of Victorian security were being shattered by the discoveries of science and the contracting certitudes of religion. Salvation was being sought in dietary reform, eurhythmics, and garden city experiments.

In a few weeks, Newnes's 'Vegetarian Company's Saloon' had a turnover enabling him to sell at a net profit of £400. As a postscript to the venture, his brother-in-law, James Hillyard, recalled that one day he went there to look for Newnes, who was not in. He was lunching in a chop-house in another part of the city. 'Everyone to his fancy,' he remarked, eyes twinkling.

That was the Manchester of silk hats and cloth caps, of cobbles and shawls, of broughams and brewers' drays, a city of stone and iron echoing the intimidating clangour of the industrial revolution. A time-and-smoke stained city of powerful opinions animating global politics and more than local reforms. Of frock-coated directors dictating letters through cigar haze to subservient male secretaries accomplished in copper-plate handwriting. Of masterful men from the ranks whose tyrannies gave urgency to the rise of trades-unionism. Of opulent grillrooms where the Continental waiters were expected to make sense of some of the ugliest regional speech in the kingdom. Of street stalls trafficking in black puddings and vinegary sea foods. Festering under the raucous prosperity, out at Ancoats, for instance, was some of the nation's direst poverty. Co-existing with both, a formidable appreciation of the arts that ensured Manchester's status as one of the provincial capitals of Europe.

2

Newnes was all business briskness and bustle. His blue eyes flashed with purpose as he talked, a man who preferred to work in his shirtsleeves when he was not 'on the road', and who put his feet up only at the end of a twelve-hour day. Finance apart, it would have meant no special effort for him to get the first issue of his paper ready for press in days rather than weeks. If his final decision to publish it came as late as August 1881 after reading the little piece about the train mishap, he was quite capable of acting in conformity with the newly imported American motto that he had made his own: *Do it now*. Like many men of exceptional energy, he was flatteringly misjudged by those who were deficient in that respect. He was not a genius or a specially gifted man. There was nothing about him that was larger than life, not even his dreams.

No. 1 of *Tit-Bits From All the Most Interesting Books, Periodicals and Newspapers In The World*, was dated October 22, 1881, 'published for the proprietor, George Newnes, of Sunnyside, Stretford, in the County of Lancashire', and printed by William Evans, 3 Cross Street, Manchester. Sixteen pages no cover, no illustrations, no advertisements. Its flat columns of dirty type were broken only by single-line headings similar to those with which he had become familiar in the local evening paper: *A Strange Hobby*, *Anecdotes of Gamblers*, *Curious Epitaphs*, *Incidents at the Siege of Lucknow*, *How Our Queen Was Wooed*. Nothing there to suggest that the spirit of the age hovered over the flatbed presses whence *Tit-Bits* came. As for the paper being a mainspring of mighty developments, that would have seemed ridiculous. It still does.

Five thousand copies were sold in two hours, largely with the help of a squad of newsboys wearing hatbands that identified them as 'The *Tit-Bits* Brigade' as they marched up and down Market Street, Manchester. Streets were then the principal areas of exta-mural publicity. Newspaper display

advertising did not yet exist. Up in Glasgow, Thomas Lipton, the chain-store grocer, was having mammoth Canadian cheeses drawn by a traction-engine, and once by an elephant, from the docks to his warehouse. It made people talk. That was Newnes's intention too.

The manager of W. H. Smith's bookstall at Victoria Station, Manchester, said that, seeing a first copy of *Tit-Bits*, he made up his mind to 'push it', because he thought it might provide much-needed opposition to 'the blood-and-thunders', which had led Smith's to consider compiling their subsequently effective black list. *Tit-Bits* had in its favour that it came out on Saturday for Sunday reading. Newnes was shocked and hurt when he heard that some people bought the paper because its title had a meaning that produced giggles in the music-halls. To them, a tit-bit was an off-colour anecdote, while in some other vocabularies it had a sex connotation. There was awkward sales resistance on that account at Newcastle-upon-Tyne. When Newnes went there to investigate, he was firmly told by the local newsagents: 'It won't go. People don't like the name.'

The last stronghold of Newcastle obduracy was a woman newsvendor who had a large sales round with many customers who relied on her personal recommendation of the papers they took in. 'What she did not approve, they rejected,' Newnes wrote. She was entirely critical of the title of his paper. 'She said it wasn't decent.' Making no impression on her himself, Newnes sent his brother-in-law, Hillyard, to see her. Hillyard told her: 'Mr Newnes's wife is my sister. Do you think she would have married the sort of man you seem to think he is? I tell you—never!' It was the end of Newcastle opposition to the advent of *Tit-Bits*.

Four different firms printed the paper in its first few weeks: Evans of Cross Street, Manchester; W. T. Emmott of the Black-friars Printing Works, Salford; Abel Haywood of the Excelsior Printing Works; and Taylor, Garnett & Co., of Warren Street, Manchester. Those frequent changes suggest that Newnes's path was not smooth at the beginning. A former chairman of Emmott's, W. H. Spurr, who was with the company 66 years, stated that 'on one occasion, Mr W. T. Emmott, the founder of the firm, refused the property in *Tit-Bits* as payment of a debt arising from its printing'.[1]

Before a year was out, the tide turned. *Tit-Bits* was set for success. Its sales mounted to five, then six figures. The Manchester business man who disdained the chance of securing a half-share in it for £500 now came forward with an offer of £16,000 for an outright purchase, which Newnes declined. In the same period, seven new publications came on the market in the mould and form of his devising. The first was mischievously called *Rarebits*. Within twelve months the number grew to twenty-two. None made real headway or seriously interfered with his progress and most soon fell out of the running. When his circulation bounded well beyond the hundred thousand mark, Newnes received an offer of £30,000. That, too, he refused.

By no recondite design, he had introduced into journalism a formula that allied it with the coming technological advances, showing that food for the mind could be processed and packaged like food for the body. Kellogg's cornflakes and Newnes's literary snacks: both were early manifestations of an irresistible trend.

He remarked to his brother-in-law in an awesome tone: 'I believe I'm going to be rich.' He had moments of 'being frightened by success'. In one of them he seriously thought that, after all, he would sell out. For one brought up in the manse, sudden wealth had bedevilling undertones. Conscience had to be appeased by religious sanctions, by demonstrations of practical concern for the good of others: service in Parliament; benefactions to Matlock Bath, where he was born; a fully equipped Free Library for Putney, where he made his London home; a cliff railway for Lynton, where he spent his holidays. Assured of prosperity, he went back to call on the elderly couple who had tended him after his fall in the street. He wished them to know that his gratitude went deeper than words. He showed it by buying them an annuity.

[1] Information supplied by Messrs Emmott & Co., Ltd., in a letter of February 23, 1961.

3

'What truth does this promote, moral or political?' It would hardly have occurred to Newnes that his scatterbrain publication should comply with either of those Johnsonian alternatives, though he might fairly have claimed that he was imbued by a desire for the betterment of the people. His chief aim as a publisher was to provide information as entertainment; for the time being, his aspirations soared no higher. His business sense was more acute than his editorial flair.

A circulation spreading fast beyond its local bounds obliged him to transfer his activities to London four years after he began publishing in Manchester, during which time he resigned his job as a fancy-goods representative. At first, he used an accommodation address for letters at 152 Fleet Street. He then rented a floor in a ramshackle building in Farringdon Street, E.C., where his desk was a trestle table.

In June 1886, he moved the offices of *Tit-Bits* to Burleigh Street, a short and crowded confluent of the Strand, where the smell of printer's ink mingled with assorted aromas of Covent Garden Market. Clustered there already were the offices of several publications *The Globe*, the *Guardian*, *Church News*, and the *Court Journal*. Newnes's office, still there, was part of the parsonage of St Michael's (Episcopal) Church. His neighbour at No. 5 was William Odhams, a printer whose family name was to become as prominent as Newnes's in the publishing industry. A few yards down on the left-hand side, where Exeter Street cuts across Burleigh Street, was the stage door of the Lyceum Theatre, the scene of Sir Henry Irving's triumphs. Opposite was Exeter Hall, focal point of Evangelical controversy and the arena of Fabian Society debates, obliterated these many years since by the Strand Palace Hotel. A stone's throw eastward were the squalid alleys and courts of Clare Market, where John Cassell had preached against drink and other social evils and where the picks and shovels of a series of Strand Improvement Schemes were at last making way for the grandiose climax of Aldwych and Kingsway.

4

Newnes entered the House of Commons in 1885 as Liberal member for Newmarket. When he went to receive the congratulations of his widowed mother, she raised her head from her sickbed pillow to exclaim: 'Oh, George, I wish you had come to tell me you were a minister.' His only distinction as an M.P. was to be nominated 'one of the best dressed men in the House'. He wrote a note of the scene in 1886 when the Commons divided over Gladstone's Home Rule Bill. 'The excitement was indescribable. Pale men were flushed, and red-faced men turned pale as the fatal moment arrived. Every man was nervously anxious, and very many were visibly trembling. I noticed that many greetings were not returned, so absorbed were men in their feelings.'

He was the first periodical publisher to apply shop window-dressing techniques to his circulation campaigns; for example, his free insurance for readers, which introduced a competitive element in publishing that long outlasted his time. 'The intense and sometimes unseemly "free insurance" battles between the popular newspapers of the 1930s, in which the benefits offered to the individual readers rose as high as £10,000, were in direct line from the *Tit-Bits* scheme of the 1880s.'[1] His prize competitions were a nine-days' wonder that sold his paper more widely than its standard contents, though his Christmas Numbers, written almost entirely by readers tempted by the guineas he offered for their contributions on seasonable themes, were household events. For one of his competitions, the General Post Office delivered three hundred mailbags full of entries.

He announced a 'hidden treasure' hunt for five hundred gold sovereigns buried at a site in the Hertfordshire country-side, indicated by clues scattered through a *Tit-Bits* serial story. 'You may call it cheap journalism,' he replied to a challenge about the propriety of encouraging the lottery spirit, 'but I will tell you this. An enormous class of superficial readers, who crave for light reading, would read the so-called sporting papers if there were no *Tit-Bits* to entertain them. At

[1] *Northcliffe* (Cassell, 1959).

A RUNAWAY TRAIN.

On Sunday evening, about nine o'clock, a train of eight carriages was being shunted at Halstead Station, on the South-Eastern Railway, and started down the incline on the road to London without the engine, which was not on the train at the time. It continued its course, and increased its speed as it ran through Chelsfield, Orpington, Chislehurst, and other stations on the road to London. A telegram was sent to all stations, and, at the junction above New Cross, the signalman, with great presence of mind, put over the points, and sent the train into the sidings to Bricklayers' Arms goods station, where it continued its rapid pace through the network of sidings and roads, and reached the locomotive department, where it ran into a dead road, knocked down a wall, and entered the premises of Messrs. Oastler and Palmer, tanners, doing great damage to a wooden building and a quantity of machinery therein. Two carriages were completely smashed, and others more or less damaged. The *débris* was speedily cleared away. It is very remarkable that this train travelled 14 miles in 17 minutes without the aid of an engine, a time which is certainly without precedent. Five children belonging to the station-master at Halstead had a marvellous escape. They were in the centre of the train, and travelled with it to London, and received a severe shaking, but in no other way were they any the worse for their adventure. Their father followed from Halstead on the engine which should have been with the train, and it is needless to say was overjoyed upon finding his children unhurt.

Here, for the first time, is reproduced the item from the *Manchester Evening News* of August 24, 1881, on which George Newnes based his idea for a new weekly to be called *Tit-Bits*. Its impact on the world of print and publication was remarkable. 'Ye gods!' exclaimed a writer in the *Caxton Magazine*, 'If there had been no *Tit-Bits*, it is likely that there would have been no *Daily Mail*, no *Daily Express*!' R. A. Scott James wrote in *The Influence of the Press* (1913): '*Tit-Bits* marked the commencement of a new era in the history of the English Press and of the English nation.'

Sir George Newnes, Bart., from the cartoon by *Spy*.

least its contents are wholesome and many of those readers may be led to take an interest in higher forms of literature.' He could have claimed, too, that a number of subsequently famous writers were glad to take guineas from *Tit-Bits* in their early days. Lord Randolph Churchill was said to have referred to *Tit-Bits* as 'the greatest literary fluke of the century'. His more than glancing intellect might later have been persuaded that the journalism of the paragraph tended to confirm in the mass mind a prejudice against mental effort and that simplification carried too far can become falsification.

Newnes's earnest personal attitude was expressed in his scrutiny of every line printed in his paper, down to the joke 'fillers' at the foot of the columns. His last-minute censorship was a trial to the staff, anxious about press times. He blue-pencilled a query about kissing in public, writing against it on the page proof: 'We should avoid any subject that may have an injurious effect on our readers.'

He was persuaded by an advertising agent, T. B. Browne, of Queen Victoria Street, E.C., to put a green cover on *Tit-Bits*. The effect was felt at once. Soon, Newnes was banking £200 a week for himself. His income was more than doubled when he set up his own advertising department. His income from *Tit-Bits* in 1890 was just under £30,000.

'I am the average man,' he would say. 'I don't have to put myself in his place. I am in his place. I know what he wants.' In his grey frock coat with its silk-faced lapels, a grey silk cravat neatly rumpled under his badger-brown beard, horn-rimmed eyeglasses suspended over his double-breasted waistcoat, he made nonsense of that assertion. He was an almost offensively comfortable-looking *entrepreneur*, replete with the artfully controlled self-esteem that marked the successful man in whom business acumen was mingled with public spirit.

His social life was limited by an obstinate preference for the company of persons of his own class and kind. It followed that his name occurs rarely in contemporary memoirs. For years he lunched four days a week with the same small group of business friends who gathered at the Hotel Cecil in the Strand. He was an accomplished chess player who met and defeated champions and conducted games over the Atlantic cable from the headquarters of the British Chess Club at 37 King Street, Covent Garden (now the Savage Club).

An acquaintance noted that he had 'the eye of a sailor, clear and physically far-seeing'. What most impressed C. B. Fry, the Oxford scholar-athlete who became one of England's cricket immortals, was Newnes's 'rare capacity for thinking a subject through'. Fry saw him as essentially 'a retiring man', whose uncomplicated mental processes took him straight to the heart of the matter without waste of words. His voice seemed to come from his chest. His speaking style was deliberate and often homiletic.

His remembered echoing laugh was prompted more often by his own jokes than by those of other people. He thought it amusing to write as an advertisement for his paper: 'The height of Ben Nevis is 4,406 feet. The height of absurdity is not to read *Tit-Bits*.' Returning from Holland, he interjected into his conversation for some time afterwards the story of his being asked by a Dutchman to 'admire that hill over there', and of his retorting, 'I can't see it—there's a clothes-line in the way.'

He was domestically settled in a brick-built mansion called Wildcroft, on Putney Heath, gratified to be able to say that it was once part of a royal demesne. He drove to and from his Strand office in a brougham. His son Frank said that his father 'wore out several horses' in the course of those daily journeys at all seasons.

On March 1, 1889, his young rival, Alfred Harmsworth, wrote to the backer of his own recent venture into publishing: 'This week's *Tit-Bits* is very bad. The Wine Merchant has been away for two months straight off. Perhaps it is the effect of that stuff he has drunk for the past eight years.' It was true that Newnes had acquired an interest in a West End wine business and that there were rumours of his having been seen under the influence of drink. Some of his office colleagues believed that he had not recovered from the shock of the death of his elder son Arthur, aged eight. Like his father, the boy was a clever chess player. The board, with the figures in the position of the last game that they played together when he was struck down by meningitis, remained untouched on its table for years after. It was recorded that Newnes's hair turned grey, 'though he was only forty years old . . . the blow was so terrible'.

FOUR

And So—'The Strand Magazine'

Newnes was pleased to receive a suggestion for a new publication from W. T. Stead, his celebrated senior alumnus of Silcoates. Stead's term as editor of the *Pall Mall Gazette* was
coming to an end. He now wanted to bring out a magazine
which would do for educated readers what *Tit-Bits* did for
another class of person, 'to provide them', as he stated it, 'with
time-saving reading which represents the scattered wisdom
and opinion of the civilised world'. To objections that there
were more periodicals than there was time for reading them,
Stead made reply: 'That is why I am adding another to the
list, not as a rival but as a guide to those already in existence.'
It was a kind of journalism that reached its apogee in the
Reader's Digest. He proposed as the title: *The Sixpenny Magazine: A Review of Reviews*.

With Newnes's backing, the first issue was ready in four
weeks, reaching the bookstalls in January 1890. No doubt
wisely, Newnes had persuaded him to change the name of
the magazine to the *Review of Reviews*. Public interest in
what a learned professor alluded to as 'Stead's boiled magazine'
was heightened by the widely advertised welcome given to it
by the Archbishop of York, Cardinal Manning, Lord Chief
Justice Coleridge, Mr Gladstone and Lord Tennyson. Securing
that imposing patronage was Stead's triumph. Newnes's good
standing as his partner was not likely to have been overlooked.
'Have had no writs at present!' Newnes appended to a letter
written on January 10, 1890.

Behind the jaunty postscript was a hint of nervousness
about Stead's excitable judgment that before long was to flare
up into a crisis state. Stead proposed to print a letter from

Mrs Annie Besant, the Theosophist. Newnes feared that it would 'shut the *Review* out of numberless homes'. More worry over an article that might have provoked a writ for libel from *The Times*, though Sir George Lewis, the solicitor, advised that there was little risk of it, gave Newnes sleepless nights. By the end of six months he decided to retire from the partnership with Stead. Protesting that he was not a man of means, Stead raised £3,000, bought Newnes's interest in the *Review of Reviews*, and went his way. At their parting, Newnes addressed Stead in pulpit tones about their divergent views.

'There is one kind of journalism which directs the affairs of nations. It makes and unmakes Cabinets. It upsets governments, builds up navies and does many other great things. It is magnificent. That is your journalism. There is another kind of journalism which has no such great ambitions. It is content to plod on, year after year, giving wholesome and harmless entertainment to crowds of hard-working people craving for a little fun and amusement. It is quite humble and unpretentious. That is my journalism.'[1] He might have quoted De Quincey's classification of 'the literature of information' as against that of power.

2

The severance from Stead left Newnes with another sort of problem. He had engaged for the *Review of Reviews* an editorial staff which Stead could not afford to take with him. Newnes was not a man of arbitrary temper. He was considerate in his treatment of employees. He kept his *Review of Reviews* staff on the payroll while he pondered what to do.

Precisely how his new monthly illustrated magazine, 'to cost sixpence and be worth a shilling', originated is a matter of conflicting records. Newnes's biographer[1] says that he evolved it after studying the American magazines that were invading the British market with some success. A later and possibly more exact account stated explicitly that the idea was brought to him by H. Greenhough Smith, a member of the editorial staff of *Temple Bar*, one of London's older

[1] Hulda Frederichs: *The Life of Sir George Newnes* (1911).

and stodgier magazines. Newnes himself said that some of the American magazines, *Harper's*, *Scribner's*, the *Atlantic Monthly*, the *Century*, were 'smarter, livelier and more interesting', and that he feared that 'they might supplant those of native birth', meaning *The Cornhill*, *Cassell's*, and others bearing the names of London publishing houses, Bentley, Macmillan, Longmans, and Chapman & Hall. None of them, American or English, had a circulation that impressed him as the proprietor of a weekly paper selling by the hundred thousand.

There is no doubt that Newnes's judgment and final decision were influenced by *Harper's* and *Scribner's*. The format of both was typographically dignified and embellished by the best that American illustrators could provide. They were admirable productions of their time. He emerged from his ruminative phase with the conviction that there was a chance for a British magazine with 'a picture on every page'. No magazine anywhere had yet carried illustration that far. Technically, as he soon found, it was not then practical. He modified his plan to allow for a picture at every opening of the magazine, which was novelty enough.

There was nothing to frustrate his resolve that the magazine should be organically complete each month, 'like a book'. It meant dropping the serial stories that were a feature of other magazines, including the American, and relying for fiction exclusively on short stories. They were a literary form in which few English writers then excelled. There was no English equivalent of Maupassant in France, or of Ambrose Bierce in America. English short story writers were in thrall to a convention of length, six thousand words minimum. A writer submitting a story of lesser length had almost no chance of acceptance. Editors counted on stories to fill a given number of pages. A similar rule governed the length of leading articles in the newspapers. They were written to fill a column, no more, no less.

Ignoring Andrew Lang's stricture that 'the famed foreigners, Dostoievsky, and M. Zola, and M. de Maupassant often seem to be in the mood when man delights them not, nor woman either', Newnes looked to the Continent to supply him with good short stories, whatever their length. Thus it came to be written of him that 'he exerted a popular influence of great importance in that lively period of English story-telling which reached its height in the 'nineties'.[1]

He called his new magazine *The Strand* after rejecting various alternatives. (It nearly became *The Burleigh Street Magazine*.) 'The name of a periodical does not really matter so much as people imagine. If you can put such material into the pages as will attract the public, they become so accustomed to the name that after a while it really signifies very little whether the title be a good or bad one.'[2] Greenhough Smith recalled: 'We had four months to get the magazine ready in. We had no stories, no articles, no contracts for paper or printing.'[3]

A freelance artist, G. H. Haite, later one of the founders of the London Sketch Club, was invited to submit a cover design. His finally approved foreshortened impression of the Strand in the '90s, with the clock tower of the new Royal Courts of Justice showing beyond the two 'wedding cake' church towers of St Clement Danes and St Mary-le-Strand, its top hats undulant under the sun-blinds, its radial telegraph wires, the newsboys, the hansom cab, the big round gas globe pendant from No. 359 Strand at the corner of Burleigh Street, showed that in him the period had a most persuasive servitor with pen and brush. *The Strand Magazine* cover became a venerated example of popular art.

3

'A somewhat dull year.' So wrote a reputable social historian as he surveyed the passing show of 1891.[4] It included the *cause célèbre* of the year, the Tranby Croft baccarat scandal, which provided the spectacle of the Heir to the Throne being cross-examined in the witness box. For George Newnes 1891 was *annus mirabilis*, no less. His business was formed into

[1] *The Times*, December 14, 1949.
[2] Sir George Newnes: autobiographical notes.
[3] H. Greenhough Smith: *World's Press News*, December 18, 1930.
[4] R. H. Gretton: *A Modern History of the English People*.

a private limited liability company, 'with a view to consolidate [sic] the undertaking and to enable the Trade and the Advertisers in the various publications to participate in its prosperity'. As a result, newsagents and booksellers all over the country became directly concerned with the Newnes company's affairs.

He had another reason for self-congratulation. He had found a success formula for the second time, an exhilarating experience for anyone operating in the mercurial realm of ideas. He looked back on it with gusto. 'Man alive! What days those were and how we worked!' His *Strand Magazine*, with its 112 pages of articles and stories, its relatively lavish illustration, its free coloured print of a favourite picture from the previous year's Royal Academy, its advertising pages burgeoning with the signs of prosperity, sold 300,000 copies of its first issue, priced sixpence, dated January 1891, including a 'special reprint' priced at one shilling.

No other magazine, British or American, approached that circulation, infinitesimal though it now seems. A final sale of nearly half a million copies a month was achieved within a comparatively short time and held through many years. The growth of railway travel was a considerable factor in that success. *The Strand Magazine* was an evergreen best-seller at all the main line bookstalls and most of the lesser ones.

Editorially, the magazine bore the marks of a hasty compilation rather than of artful planning, a comment that could be fairly applied to the first six numbers. The stories by Balzac, Pushkin, Mérimée, Lermontoff, Dumas, Sienkiewicz, could not be considered the pick of the best that the Continent was producing. Nor were the writers in English in any sense superior: J. E. Preston Muddock ('Dick Donovan'); E. W. Hornung, who had not yet created Raffles; W. Clark Russell; Bret Harte. An anonymous short story, *The Voice of Science*, struck a note of novelty by making a phonograph indispensable to the plot, giving it an ingenious twist. Turning to the index, we find that the author was A. Conan Doyle.

On the factual side, too, there were signs of a hurried rallying of ideas and of pictures to illustrate them. *The Metropolitan Fire Brigade* and *How the Blind are Educated* did not indicate the lively invention usually associated with new publications. Yet critical comment showed that for some tastes the new magazine was 'too American'. *The Review of Reviews* referred to it as 'a cross between French and American monthlies'. If *Harper's* and *Scribner's*, for example, helped to give substance to Newnes's dream of magazine success, he could have argued that there was a two-way indebtedness, that the leading American magazines had gained from the work of English authors, from Dickens to Mrs Humphry Ward, from Thackeray to Hardy. In 1950, *Harper's* paid tribute to 'the wonderful English serial novels' that ran through the early volumes of that magazine. Newnes could have gone further and claimed that *The Strand* was the progenitor of popular illustrated magazine production in the United States. *Munsey's* was started in October 1891, nine months after *The Strand*. *McClure's* followed in 1893. Both were powerful contenders in the field and both quickly established a lead over the older American magazines, just as *The Strand* did in the British market.

4

Tit-Bits identified Newnes with the broad base of the English class pyramid. *The Strand Magazine* was a passport to recognition at higher social altitudes. An ingratiating feature, *Portraits of Celebrities at Different Times of Their Lives*, guaranteed him valuable new goodwill among eminent persons of the time. He explained to his readers: 'Some portraits of Sir Richard Webster, Q.C., at a country house, first suggested the notion of this series, which has proved so popular.' So popular that the series ran continuously through every issue for the next seven years, and was renewed intermittently, giving it a total span of sixteen years, beginning with Lord Tennyson and ending with Lloyd George.

Those two not utterly disparate personalities were the flanking pillars of a fascinating gallery of period portraits. It combined the picturesque sterility of Madame Tussaud's with the snobbish self-esteem of *Who's Who*. Deference was accorded alike to lasting and fleeting fame. The tone throughout was cloyingly civil. Women's ages were a topic of editorial discretion. Generally, they were withheld. The same degree of delicacy was observed in the case of certain actors, necessarily sensitive to the effect of time on their reputations.

Public prominence was the watchword. It justified the daring (and, as it chanced, posthumous) inclusion of Charles Bradlaugh, the atheist M.P., who was reviled also for his unyielding support of Indian national aspirations. Critics were forestalled by references to his 'doubtless erroneous opinions', his sincerity and abilities, 'the goodness of his heart'. The choice of him as a subject was doubtless sanctioned by Newnes's Liberal prejudices. In that pantheon of ruthless respectability it still strikes a discordant note.

Portraits of Celebrities conferred on *The Strand* much of its early prestige. It enabled the advertising manager to insinuate in his letters to prospective space buyers that 'Lord Tennyson has had the kindness to assist us in choosing his portraits', and that Mr Beerbohm Tree, Sir John Millais, R.A., Mr Gladstone, and Cardinal Manning, had been 'most obliging'. It was the editor, not the advertising manager, who noted that 'this page enables one to trace the blooming of the Jersey Lily (Mrs Langtry) from the bud to the full flower'. Aspects of her full flowering, subsequently disclosed in memoirs, would have shocked those *Strand* readers who gazed on her demure sweetness portrayed at the ages of 18, 23, and 'the present day' (age unstated).

The portraits used as illustrations continued to be 'engraved from photographs' right up to 1898, although the new half-tone process of photographic reproduction was experimented with on other pages in the first issue in 1891, since when it had made rapid headway. In America, *Scribner's* for June 1891 published striking examples of the new method. Three years later in London, a new weekly, *The Sketch*, had an *avant-garde* success with its half-tone pictures of famous actresses printed direct from metal blocks. Photographic blocks began to be used regularly in *The Strand* from 1893.

Meanwhile, *Portraits of Celebrities* pursued its successful course assisted by the camera at secondhand. In doing so, it helped to make the reputations of the London studio photographers, Elliot & Fry of Baker Street, Bassano of Old Bond Street, and W. & D. Downey of Ebury Street, who supplied the original photographs from which the engravings were made and who regularly received printed acknowledgment of their services. The series was finally illustrated by photographs from 1905 onward.

It was George Newnes's boast that *The Strand Magazine* 'created and enhanced many reputations in the art world'. For him, that meant the popular illustrators, a race of men who were less nervous than the wood engravers about what the coming of the camera might mean to them. The names that would have sprung readily to his mind in asserting that claim were Haite, Paget, Millar, Hardy, Browne, Shepperson, Woollen, Brock, Forestier, Sullavan, Pearse, Shepherd, and Boot, all associated with *The Strand* from the beginning.

H. R. Millar, from Thornhill, Dumfriesshire, *via* Birmingham Municipal School of Art, who spun delicate webs of fancy as the illustrator of the Shakespeare comedies, said that his best work was done for *The Strand*. Paul Hardy, from Bath, 'bearded like the corsair', and boldly aggressive with pen and brush, illustrated many of the translated short stories by European writers. W. B. Woollen, from the Slade, epitomised in line and wash the exploits of Brigadier Gerard, the new fiction character evolved by Conan Doyle for *The Strand* to succeed Sherlock Holmes.

The work of Gordon Browne, son of 'Phiz' (Hablot K. Browne), Dickens's illustrator, C. E. Brock, A. Forestier, A. Pearse and J. A. Sullavan, soon became familiar to readers. J. A. Shepherd, a *Punch* artist, enslaved them with his delightfully eccentric drawings for *Zig-Zags at the Zoo*, a famous *Strand* series invented after the artist had attended a barn dance at Horley, Surrey, where he lived and worked. Another well-remembered name was F. Carruthers Gould, the Devonian stockbroker cartoonist chiefly responsible for sustaining the monocled image of Joseph Chamberlain in the public mind. His drawing was stiff and stilted but he rarely missed a likeness. He supplied the sketches for *The Strand* feature called *From Behind The Speaker's Chair*, which annotated every session of Parliament through many years.

The art editor, W. J. K. Boot, R.I., was vice-president of the Royal Society of British Artists. His services to *The Strand* over more than twenty years may not have been recognised as they deserved. His contribution to its early reputation was substantial. Through him, twenty of the leading black-and-white artists found constant employment for the next ten years.

The succession during the '90s and after included many other accomplished and in some instances celebrated exponents of a branch of art distinguished by a respect for drawing more wholehearted than it has been at any time since. Their reputations were not made overnight or by the manipulations of publicity. They worked as if they were impelled by a belief that art exists not for the intellectual enrichment of the few but for the frank enjoyment of all. They subscribed to the doctrine of John Addington Symonds, that 'it should be the purpose of all good craftsmen not to weaken but to fortify; not to dispirit and depress, but to exalt and animate'. Pedlars of humour, sentiment, and beauty, they kept the theme of art fresh in many minds.

They were not discountenanced by the critical argument that, apart from techniques, illustration can be bad art because it is superfluous, that a storyteller or a poet who has something to say does not need an artist to help him say it. They could have answered fairly, if tangentially, that the widening use of illustrations in magazines on both sides of the Atlantic was an important influence in forming taste, in leading the public to accept values superior to those of the shoddy chromo-lithographs invented by Senefelder in 1796, that had long been the common denominator of art appreciation among the masses.

While some of the popular illustrators seemed to have been hynotised by Du Maurier's *Trilby* into stylising the women in their drawings, in general they were impervious to the art vogues, which tended increasingly to disparage draughtsman-ship. There was nothing dubious about their self-expression, even when they drew their inspiration from ebullient sessions at the Langham Sketching Club or the London Sketch Club, where they munched celery and drank beer between the life and landscape classes. Some of them brought to the pages of *The Strand* the finest traditions of book illustration, of which the period saw a splendid flowering.

5

The Strand did not make a fetish of 'big names' as a circulation lure. It concentrated on readability, a policy noted with approval by *The Bookman*, the new monthly published by Hodder & Stoughton. Most of the early writers for *The Strand* had no public reputation.

Among its contributors from the beginning was Arthur Morrison (1863–1945), whose sketches of life in London's East End, collected in *Tales of Mean Streets*, and two novels, *A Child of the Jago* and *The Hole in the Wall*, have since become prominent on the paperback shelves as minor Victorian classics. He wrote a number of carefully researched articles for the magazine and provided the text for the popular series, *Zig-Zags at the Zoo*.

The Civil Service in the last few years of the nineteenth century seemed to produce as many successful men of letters as distinguished public servants. That circumstance was subacidly noted in *The Bookman* at the time. 'The gentlemen of the Civil Service, for the payment of whose salaries we poor literary folk are taxed, are prominent among literary producers. Though a grateful country employs (or believes it employs) their energies from 10 a.m. to 4 p.m., they still have sufficient intellectual and physical force—lucky men!— to turn out, at their leisure, a remarkable variety of publications, on which, apparently, a good deal of research has been bestowed. The public would probably be surprised to learn how many of the names best known to them in current literature are those of men who draw comfortable salaries from the public purse.'

The salary was evidently not comfortable enough for Arthur Morrison, a Kentish man who worked on the staff of the Charity Commission. He left to take his chance as a freelance journalist, at first writing on cycling topics for the Iliffe printing and publishing firm at Coventry, where one of his editors was young Alfred Harmsworth. He then joined W. E. Henley in the belligerent Tory journalism of the *National Observer*. On its collapse, he worked on freelance terms for *Macmillan's Magazine* and also for *Tit-Bits*, one of those contributors who helped to justify Dr Robertson Nicoll's estimate of that weekly as 'a really useful, entertaining, and inoffensive periodical'. Morrison could always be counted on to do the best that was required of him.

He was the first writer to mould a fiction detective in the image of Sherlock Holmes. His Martin Hewitt was at the head of the procession formed up behind Conan Doyle and having in its ranks Paul Trent, Inspector French, Dr Thorndyke, Lord Peter Wimsey, Hercule Poirot. In writing ability, Morrison was superior to Conan Doyle and all but possibly one other in that line of succession.

The monument to his reputation is what remains of the old East End alley life, where spluttering gas lamps survive to cast older shadows across the pavement and memories of Jack the Ripper are not a finally banished horror of the midnight fog. Much of the violence that Morrison commemorated has gone from the streets, along with the stews and the stench. But there are still rats in the wainscots, and reeling men on Saturday nights, and naphtha flares among the butchers' carcases. And in the river of faces flowing down the Whitechapel Road he would recognise still many of the types that he pinned to the page with Hogarthian truth. There are few scenes in Dickens to rival that moment in *A Child of the Jago* when the father answers from the dock, in reply to the judge's formal question, has he anything to say before sentence of death is passed: 'No, sir—I done it. On'y 'e was a worse man than me!'

Tales of Mean Streets, considered a 'strong' book in its time, upset squeamish philanthropists by the degrading miseries it revealed. Some thought it heartless in the severity of its disclosures of the lives of the poor. It was a powerful reinforcement of the realism of George Gissing, George Moore and Richard Whiteing. In 1902, the library of *H.M.S. Ophir*, in which the future King George V sailed round the world, was sold at auction in King Street, Covent Garden. One of the books was *Tales of Mean Streets*. On the flyleaf was written: 'This is very powerful. George.'

Morrison's experience of East End life was gained at first-hand in the course of his work for the Charity Commission. The information he wanted was more than statistical and to procure it he became a matchbox maker, working at a factory bench. He was well up in boxing lore and by means of it he was admitted to clubs where the criminal element was strong. Five years of contacts with the depraved poor left him with an apparently inflexible belief that permanent reform was a vain dream. Everything that he wrote was stamped with informed pessimism. It was no mere temperamental reaction. It was the result of deliberate self-communion, drawing on ripe knowledge.

Morrison stopped writing soon after the First World War, his career rounded off by a two-volume study of Japanese art, which fascinated him. His collection of Japanese prints, which he acquired by meeting incoming ships at London docks and buying specimens from the crews, was finally sold to the British Museum for a five-figure sum, assuring him a retirement that he might not have gained by his writing.

That I had opportunities of talking with him, though only in his last years, is one of my remembered pleasures. He was proud of his association with 'the old *Strand*', and was not discomfited to recall that it was he who had gone out with Sir George Newnes's son Frank to a crossroads near Hatfield to bury the five hundred gold sovereigns for the *Tit-Bits* treasure hunt. 'They were hidden in two iron tubes, which we drove into the verge close to the high road. A man named Hubbard, from Leicester, rode straight to the spot on his bicycle and recovered the sovereigns well ahead of everybody else.' Morrison wrote the *Tit-Bits* serial that contained the clues.

My mental image of him is coloured by his time-rouged cheekbones, on which rested the gold-rimmed *pince-nez* which he looked over rather than through. There was a hint of the sage about him, and it was not necessarily derived from his preoccupation with Oriental art. He was a quietly companionable man who talked with the authority of distinguished reminiscence. As one of the redoubtable Henley's 'young men' on the *National Observer*, he knew Kipling and Wells, Barrie and Yeats, and had sat at the dinner tables of some of the era's leading hostesses. He told me of Edmund Gosse referring to Marie Corelli as 'that little milliner'. Morrison said that it was 'the most opprobrious remark that could be made about a woman at that time'.

The first issues of *The Strand Magazine* were published from *Tit-Bits* office in Burleigh Street, Strand, London, in a building that still exists.

A. Conan Doyle in the early '90s, when he was writing the first series of Sherlock Holmes adventures.

Sidney Paget, the illustrator of Sherlock Holmes, whose drawings did much to fix Holmes in the public mind.

An illustration by Sidney Paget for *The Adventure of the Abbey Grange*, in the second Sherlock Holmes series (September 1904).

FIVE

Enter Sherlock Holmes

I

Two short stories, submitted on foolscap in small plump handwriting, arrived on the desk of Greenhough Smith, who had been appointed literary editor of the new magazine. Forty years later he described how he reacted on that day in the late spring of 1891. 'I at once realised that here was the greatest short story writer since Edgar Allan Poe. I remember rushing into Mr Newnes's room and thrusting the stories before his eyes.'

The self-perpetuation of Greenhough Smith as a creature of impulse is amusingly at variance with one's impression of him in his later years. It was hardly confirmed by his dry, sparing smile and clinically detached manner that suggested recondite inner resources. Earlier he had explained: 'Good story-writers were scarce, and here, to an editor jaded with wading through reams of impossible stuff, comes a gift from Heaven, a god-send in the shape of a story that brought a gleam of happiness into the despairing life of this weary editor. Here was a new and gifted story-writer: there was no mistaking the ingenuity of the plot, the limpid clearness of the style, the perfect art of telling a story.'

The two stories that seized his attention that day bore as their respective titles *A Scandal in Bohemia* and *The Red-Headed League*. Their author had appended his name and address: Dr A. C. Doyle, 2 Devonshire Place, W. They were written to correct what in his opinion was 'the great defect of most detective fiction, that the chief character arrived at his results without any obvious reason. That is not fair, it is not art.' The stories were the first of a series of six published under the collective title of *The Adventures of Sherlock Holmes*.

The Strand had not noticeably benefited from the translated short stories of Balzac, de Maupassant, Hugo, de Musset, Mérimée and Pushkin. Of the effect of *The Adventures of Sherlock Holmes* there was no question. The circulation response was as immediate and as conclusive as a reflex action. In six months, Conan Doyle's name was made as the creator of a fiction detective of infinitely wider appeal than Poe's Dupin or Gaboriau's Tabaret and Lecoq.

On August 6, 1891, Doyle wrote to Alfred Harmsworth, whose own fortunes had by then improved: 'I agree with you that the illustrations are excellent. Sidney Paget is the name.' The future Northcliffe had inquired about the artist whose visualisation of Holmes was more explicit than the few swift verbal strokes by which his originator defined him: ' . . . . a thin, razor face . . . a great hawk's-bill of a nose and two small eyes set close together'. Paget, who was brought in to do the illustrations by Boot, *The Strand* art editor, is given hardly more than a passing nod in the authorised biography of Conan Doyle.[1] Yet his idea of the appearance and style of Holmes was the model for the many subsequent characterisations on stage and screen. William Gillette, Arthur Wontner, Eille Norwood, Raymond Massey, Basil Rathbone and, more recently, Douglas Wilmer (on B.B.C. television): each, with varying degrees of fidelity, personified the Holmes of Paget's imagination rather than of Conan Doyle's.

Sidney Paget, born 1860, was the son of an official of the old Local Government Board at Clerkenwell, himself a man of mature artistic tastes. Sidney Paget was trained at Heatherley's and the Royal Academy School. He worked on his Sherlock Holmes drawings in a studio at 11 Holland Park Road, Kensington. It was the profile of one of his two artist brothers, Walter, that crystallised Holmes in his mind. His daughter Winifred remembers that when her uncle Walter attended a recital at what is now Wigmore Hall, London, 'as he walked to his seat, a woman in the audience exclaimed: "Why, there's Sherlock Holmes!"'

Whether artist and author met at that early stage is not known. Drawn by Paget, the Grand Duke of Cassel-Felstein,

[1] John Dickson Carr: *The Life of Sir Arthur Conan Doyle* (Murray, 1949).

'hereditary king of Bohemia', in the first of the *Adventures*, is strongly reminiscent of Doyle himself, who had the physical presence and authority of a personage. Paget's contribution to the Holmes legend was important, as vitally so as Seymour's linear realisation of Pickwick. Paget supplied the deerstalker cap which assisted the fixation of Sherlock Holmes in the public mind.

2

Conan Doyle's heart was in historical fiction, which another distinguished contributor to *The Strand*, Grant Allen, regarded as 'a recrudescence of barbarism and Jingo reaction'. By it Doyle hoped, and strove, to make his literary reputation. 'Holmes takes my mind from better things,' he was complaining at the end of 1891, when the *Adventures* had been running six months. He had already published *Micah Clarke*, a novel of the Western rebellion. He was finishing *The White Company*, a romance of the fourteenth century. In both, he bravely tried to restore the historical novel to the popular favour it had when Harrison Ainsworth was writing fifty years before. He did not succeed in that ambition. He considered that Charles Reade's *The Cloister and the Hearth* was the greatest achievement of its kind.

Herbert Asquith, one of the sons of the Prime Minister of a later time, played golf with Doyle in the Cotswolds. Driving home from a match, Conan Doyle 'suddenly turned his head and told me that he sometimes wished that he had never written a word about Sherlock Holmes . . . He mentioned *The White Company* as a book which he greatly preferred to his detective fiction. I think he felt that his more serious work had been put too much in the shade by the celebrity of his most famous character.'[1]

There was a sense in which as a writer he was unique. Unlike Thackeray, after writing *Esmond*, or Blackmore, having finished the last page of *Lorna Doone*, or, for that matter, Dickens after *A Tale of Two Cities*, he was able to divest himself completely of the period and atmosphere on

[1] *Moments of Memory* (Hutchinson, 1937).

which he had been concentrating and to revert, naturally and easily, to his customary *milieu* and style.

'I had called upon my friend Sherlock Holmes upon the second morning after Christmas . . . He was lounging upon the sofa in a purple dressing-gown, a pipe-rack within his reach upon the right . . . a lens and forceps lying upon the seat of the chair.'[1]

That prim insistent use of 'upon', as if 'on' were a solecism, is almost enough to put one off the Holmes trail. Fastidiousness, not to say pedantry, is subdued by an irresistible narrative force that tenses curiosity and omnipotently undertakes to satisfy it. The formula is probably as old as human consciousness. When Conan Doyle wrote to his mother on November 11, 1891, 'I think of slaying Sherlock Holmes, winding him up for good and all', she replied in a temper: 'You won't! You can't! You mustn't!' Her indignation presaged an extraordinary show of resentment by the reading public when in due time he carried out his threat.

He was paid thirty guineas each for the first set of Holmes stories in *The Strand*, and fifty guineas each for the second series. Greenhough Smith remembered him arriving silk-hatted at the office by hansom cab to deliver one of the manuscripts. A year earlier Doyle had written to Alfred Harmsworth: 'I shall be happy to do a story at the rate of £5 per thousand words, which is my present scale.' In *The Strand Magazine* account books he continued to be entered as Dr A. C. Doyle. He had given up medical practice and had gone to live at 12 Tennison Road, South Norwood, described by a *Strand* interviewer as 'a prettily-built and modest-looking red-brick residence'. He was photographed at its front door with his 'charming wife', both seated on a tandem tricycle, an inelegant machine that might have been designed to ridicule romance.

The interviewer found Doyle 'totally different from the man I expected to see', anticipating a withdrawn and introspective personality. 'He is just a happy, genial, homely man; tall, broad-shouldered, with a hand that grips you heartily, and, in its sincerity of welcome, hurts.' The photographs

[1] *The Adventure of the Blue Carbuncle.*

taken at the same time by Elliot & Fry showed that while the Doyles' income was rising, the level of their tastes was not much above that of the suburban average.

Conan Doyle 'finished with Holmes' in November 1893. Later, he wrote to a fellow novelist, David Christie Murray: 'Poor Holmes is dead and damned. I couldn't revive him if I would (at least not for years), for I have had such an overdose of him that I feel towards him as I do towards *pâté de foie gras*, of which I once ate too much . . . We have too few born story-tellers.'

The comfort of that privately confided hint of the possibility of resurrection was denied to readers who were outraged by discovering in *The Strand* for November 1893 that Holmes had been sent to presumed destruction in a Swiss cataract. 'Any attempt at recovering the bodies was hopeless, and there, deep down in that dreadful cauldron of swirling water and seething foam, will lie for all time the most dangerous criminal and the foremost champion of the law of their generation.' Having read *The Adventure of the Final Problem*, an anguished correspondent wrote to Doyle: 'You brute!'

If in protest rather than in sorrow, young City men that month put mourning crepe on their silk hats, there were others for whom the death of a myth was akin to a national bereavement. From that hour a literary cult of exceptional vitality began stirring in the womb of time. Reporting to the shareholders of his private company, of whom Conan Doyle himself was one, Newnes referred to the dispatch of Holmes as 'a dreadful event'.

He had good reason for dramatising it. The Sherlock Holmes series supplied much of the momentum that carried *The Strand Magazine* forward into the first place in magazine popularity. It meant that Doyle's reputation was as secure in the boardroom as outside it, giving him a status among the business men that was a fairly rare thing in authorship. By means of it he exercised a power, if not a right, of veto on advertising in which his name occurred. When, after Sidney Paget's death, a drawing of Holmes was made by another hand for publicity purposes, Doyle wrote to Greenhough Smith: 'It will never do. Holmes must preserve his dignity.

He looks about five feet high, badly dressed, and with no brains or character—an actor out of a job.'

Greenhough Smith never shared Doyle's indifference to the display of public concern at his hero's fate. He told readers of *The Strand*: 'Holmes seems as real as Falstaff or as Pecksniff, and much more real than Cato or King John.' Finally, Doyle wrote in exasperation: 'I am weary of his name.' Ten years were to pass before he could bring himself to accept his creation as a fiction immortal.

Others were in sympathy with Doyle's state of mind. *On Sherlock Holmes the shadows close* was a line in verses that consigned also to the limbo Du Maurier's Trilby and Kipling's Mulvaney and Ortheris.[1] One of the book pundits, Robertson Nicoll, insisted that Conan Doyle 'has lost ground since the days of his great popularity. His medical knowlege is of little help to him in his fiction. His best friends think that he is writing too quickly and turning out work too carelessly'.[2]

In inventing a new fiction character, Doyle had devised a new fiction form, the connected series of short stories, of about five or six thousand words each, that enabled readers to share the linked excitements of a serial without being committed to following every instalment. Without exception, every other popular magazine adopted it. Grant Allen gave it subtlety with his scientific imagination. Rudyard Kipling made it serve his purposes. Among the women writers, Mrs L. T. Meade exploited it with particular success.

3

Contemporaries of Conan Doyle were unanimous in their opinion of him as an eminently likeable man. He was large in heart as in build. He laughed heartily and often. He had the ungrudging esteem of his fellow writers. He championed George Moore against W. H. Smith's and Mudie's ban on *Esther Waters*. When Grant Allen was fatally stricken and unable to finish a story commissioned for the magazine, Conan Doyle undertook to write the last two thousand words for

---

[1] Edward A. Church: *A Ballade of Bygones* (1896).
[2] *The Bookman* (1896).

him. 'Difficult work,' Doyle said, 'but it was a pleasure to relieve his mind.' He marked no epoch in the history of English literature. He never qualified for high recognition in the profession of letters. He remained attached to his unaffected credo: *I have wrought my simple plan, If I give an hour of joy, To the boy who's half a man, Or the man who's half a boy.*

He could not be held accountable for the obsession with crime for crime's sake which has followed the far-spreading growth of detective fiction since his day and deriving its original impetus from a desire to emulate his success. 'You must not make the criminal a hero,' he urged his brother-in-law, E. W. Hornung, whose gentleman crook, Raffles, seemed to Doyle to be 'a kind of inversion of Sherlock Holmes'. He was not interested in the criminal mind. The introduction of the sex theme into detective story writing, with its overtones of brutishness, has since debased his ingenious, beguiling, and blameless formula.

I was told by E. N. Sanders, for twenty-nine years assistant editor of *The Strand*, that Doyle would never accept a commission for new work until what he had in hand was finished, 'down to the last word on the last page'. In 1948, Sanders wrote to me that 'no one could have known Conan Doyle over a long period without being struck by his eager zest for life and his intense devotion to the task of the moment, whether work or play. And,' added that old admirer of his, 'what a fine all-round sportsman he was in his time'!

It was a corrective tribute, induced by the disclosure of my own unfortunate impression of Conan Doyle three or four years before he passed from the world. Over literary matters I was fairly often in correspondence with him, more particularly in my role of literary editor of the *Daily Express*. He assured me, 'in the most solemn fashion', that he saw his mother and a nephew, 'years after their death as clearly as in life'. He wrote at various times complaining of the treatment of psychic subjects in the press, protesting that he was 'altogether tired' of newspaper attitudes to his investigations and informing me that he would write no more on that theme.

I went to see him at his Psychic Bookshop & Museum in

Victoria Street, S.W., almost in the shadow of Westminster Abbey. Disappointment was my lot, a depressing sentimental reverse. He was not himself. His handshake had no grip, the 'eager zest for life' was dimmed, the light turned low in his eyes. He was petulant and unheeding, treating my far from assertive questions as if they were impertinences. He appeared to be drained of generosity, once a laudable component of his nature.

What burden of the spirit had been put upon him? Something had bowed him down. Perhaps he was sharing the dismay of all who realise that time has finally borne them to the edge of the abyss. Fingering his psychic bric-a-brac, he seemed to me to be terribly ill at ease, as if he had exhausted his long-vaunted resources of comfort for mankind.

SIX

Editor for Forty Years

I

A large and, so to say, public-spirited clock with gilded numerals and hands overhangs the pavement on the east side of Southampton Street, Strand, London. It has told the time of day to two generations of passers-by, having been put there in 1897, a year of Jubilee, for the practical adornment of the new building that housed the Newnes publications. They numbered twelve, including *Woman's Life*, the first weekly of its kind. Old shops and residential premises had been pulled down, displacing by directory evidence a number of tradesmen and private tenants, among the last-named 'Israel Israel, Esq.'. The site extended back to Exeter Street, allowing for the erection of a larger building than was suggested by the frontage.

The Newnes firm that year became a public company, capitalised at £1,000,000. Young Harold Harmsworth, showing a precocious mastery of balance sheets and prospectuses, wrote to his brother Alfred: 'The actual price Newnes will receive for his business I figure out at between £600,000 and £700,000.'[1] Newnes was one of the first publishing houses to receive a Stock Exchange quotation, the company's £1 shares being marked up to £2 12s 6d in conformity with the profit trend, then exceeding £60,000 a year. Prominent in the prospectus was *The Strand Magazine*, 'which sells to the extent of 450,000 copies a month and is still growing. It has a very large circulation in America'.

Newnes, by then Sir George, was named permanent

---

[1] In 1959, George Newnes, Ltd., with its subsidiaries, including C. Arthur Pearson, Ltd., was acquired by Odhams Press, Ltd., for upwards of £12,000,000.

governing director. He was joined on the board by two friends in his Hotel Cecil circle: Lewis Tomalin, managing director of the Jaeger Clothing Company, and Edward Hudson, of the Southwark printing firm of Hudson & Kearns. When Tomalin proved to be uncongenial to certain senior members of the Newnes staff he resigned in favour of Frank Newnes, aged 22, just down from Cambridge and more ambitious to shine on the golf course than in the boardroom.

The conjunction of Sir George Newnes and Edward Hudson was a successful one. It resulted in the founding of *Country Life*, which continues to discharge with authority and to grace with dignity its role of remembrancer of our English rural heritage. Hudson is recalled by some for his huge high-roofed Rolls-Royce, with its folding steps on the running board and twin red-throated exhaust funnels on the bonnet; by others, for his daily habit of striding fearlessly across the Strand, hand imperiously upraised as a traffic signal, as he went to lunch at the Cecil or the Savoy.

Newnes had been given a baronetcy on the recommendation of Lord Rosebery, the Prime Minister, who announced that it was 'to commemorate not only your political services but the good work that you have done in the cause of healthy popular literature'. Her Majesty could have had no qualms about endorsing the honour. She had been 'graciously pleased to peruse and revise' yet another contribution to *The Strand Magazine*, and was also 'good enough to copy two pages from her Diary for this article', which dealt with her studies in Hindustani.

The article was written by 'an eminent Indian scholar' with the introductory genuflection: 'All who have read her Journals in the Highlands and her letters given to the public in the life of the Prince Consort cannot fail to find a strong literary tendency in the Imperial mind.' An article of nineteen pages on Buckingham Palace was written by 'the graciously accorded permission of Her Majesty, who allowed the writer "liberty to examine the interior".' Possibly no name in the Honours List of its year was more warmly confirmed by the approving Imperial nod than Sir George Newnes's.

As he made no mark, except sartorially, as a House of

Commons man, Newnes's political services were doubtless deemed to consist of founding the *Westminster Gazette* in the Liberal interest. It was his private venture, one which involved him in a loss of £180,000 in his five years' proprietorship. A song that was currently sung in a Gaiety Theatre musical show contained the pointed lines: *I spend a sum infernal, to support an evening journal.*

With its policy of restraint, fairness and courtesy, the *Westminster Gazette,* circulation 25,000, was one of Fleet Street's honourable failures. Its news values were as feeble as its politics were strong. It is remembered for its influential front-page leading articles by the editor, J. A. Spender, its cartoons by Sir F. Carruthers Gould, the intellectual contents of its Saturday edition, and the green-tinted paper it was printed on, intended to protect readers from eyestrain in the ill-lighted London suburban trains. Spender placed it on record that Newnes was 'always steadily against any cheapening or popularising which might have damaged the influence of the paper with its more serious readers'.

2

That was Newnes's best period, the prime of his career. The throne-room of his kingdom, with its polished mahogany panelling and its dark blue leather upholstery, gleamed in the soft glow of electroliers, the newest thing in office lighting. There was a thick pile carpet under his feet; above him, an immaculate white ceiling with mouldings picked out in salmon-pink and palest green. Striding masterfully from his desk to the windows overlooking Southampton Street, often stroking his beard upwards with the back of his hand as he did so, he looked less like a monarch of all he surveyed than an actor playing a part too hastily learnt. His make-up was convincing and he carried himself like a magnate. Yet in that relatively lush setting he seemed miscast.

Perhaps it was from an urge to shine in his under-rehearsed role that he developed a habit of exclaiming, when a proffered idea pleased him: 'That is *par excellence* what I want!' A literary researcher, summoned to his office to discuss a project, reported that Newnes flourished the phrase four times in their short interview.

Top hats hung on the door pegs of the editorial rooms and the counting house. The London telephone service could not yet provide enough lines to replace the need for messenger boys, whose hurrying feet echoed along the corridors of Southampton Street. Neither was the typewriter yet a common perquisite of business efficiency. There were no girl secretaries in the building. Sir George Newnes's young male secretary, William Plank, had the manner and some of the functions of a footman. The type was precisely exemplified by Alfred Harmsworth's first secretary, a London coachman's son named Sutton, who later blossomed as Sir George Sutton, Bart.

The rivalry between Newnes and the Harmsworths was manifested in new offices, new publications, financing Polar expeditions, in holiday trips up the Nile, in office window-box displays, in employing office boys in Eton suits at their beck and call. Newnes's office boy, William Duckworth, who became a *Daily News* reporter, wore a 'topper' on duty and claimed to have 'wiped the teacups for the leading literary figures of the day'. Alfred Harmsworth's office boy, who likewise sat dutifully outside his master's door, was his illegitimate son, the result of his alleged seduction before he was 20 by a servant girl some years older.

Newnes had no blots of that sort on his escutcheon. His baronetcy also gave him precedence over Harmsworth, who disclosed it as a personal grievance in a letter he wrote to a member of the Government in 1897, pointing out that Newnes's title had 'proved of enormous commercial advantage to him'.

Proud to pose as an art patron, Newnes opened a gallery in his new building for the display and sale to the public of original drawings used in *The Strand* as story illustrations. 'They include the work of some of our most accomplished artists.' Resolved not to be culturally outclassed, the Harmsworths made it known that the top floor of their new premises, Carmelite House, would be reserved for a permanent exhibition of contemporary art.

As a further essay in what would now be called 'public relations', Newnes invited London sightseers to visit his 'Machinery Hall' in the basement of the Southampton Street building to watch *Tit-Bits* being printed at the then phenomenal speed of 24,000 copies an hour. The brothers Harmsworth replied by issuing tickets to their shareholders and nominees to view operations at their printing works.

The competitive urge was not always uppermost. There were civil exchanges and mutual offers of help between the two rival firms when technical difficulties arose.

Soon, Newnes was confronted again by the shameless flattery of imitation, aimed at reaping where he had sown. Ward, Lock & Co., publishers of Mrs Beeton's ponderous household tome, came out with the *Windsor Magazine*, 'the biggest and best sixpennyworth ever issued'. C. Arthur Pearson, the old Wykehamist who had worked in the *Tit-Bits* office, from which he departed to launch his plagiaristic enterprise, *Pearson's Weekly*, announced *Pearson's Magazine* in the same format as *The Strand*. An existing but far from flourishing magazine, *Cassell's*, was enlarged to *The Strand* size and given a new look with an impressive array of authors' names on the cover.

The Harmsworths, who, like Pearson, might not have been in the running at all but for Newnes, entered the lists with a monthly named after them; later to become *The London Magazine*. Yet another monthly, the *Pall Mall Magazine*, had Astor money behind it. Sir George Newnes wrote in 1899: 'Most magazines are now modelled upon the plan of *The Strand Magazine*. It is not a source of annoyance but of gratification to me.'

He could afford to smile benevolently. *The Strand* continued to tower above the rest on the bookstalls, its circulation steady at half a million copies, its prestige unimpaired. Moreover, it had the advantage of an American edition, 'which has made a considerable advance in circulation during recent months' (1896).

When the tide turned, and inexorable change sounded the knell of the monthly rhythm in popular periodical publishing, it was *The Strand* that yielded last. All those others, and more, fell earlier in a battle in which there were to be no victors.

3

'Edited by Geo: Newnes' was imprinted on the cover of every volume of *The Strand* up to 1910. From the late '90s, it was a figurative assertion. By then Newnes had other interests making demands on his energies and time, among them his new *Daily Courier*, and a twopenny four-colour weekly, *The Million*, a would-be hypnotic title that proved to be devoid of suggestive force. Both were imaginative ventures, embodying many touches of originality. Both were short-lived; doom came in a few months.

Then, because exiled readers of *The Strand* submitted more articles of overseas travel and adventure than the magazine could use, he started *The Wide World Magazine*, to exploit them. Its sensational sponsorship of 'the Australian turtle rider', Louis de Rougemont, was a serious setback to its prospects, plunging Newnes into a fresh phase of anxiety, less about circulation losses than about the effect on the prestige of his company. His Arctic expedition was partly designed to re-establish it by providing *The Wide World Magazine* with unimpeachable material.

It was fortunate for *The Strand* that editorial responsibility fell more squarely on the shoulders of Greenhough Smith, for under Newnes's personal direction there was a danger of it becoming a grandiose *Tit-Bits*. As the corner-stone of his publishing house, the weekly paper had retained a strong sentimental grip on him. He continued to send for its page proofs and to keep the staff working late while he changed the make-up of the Page One jokes about mothers-in-law, seaside landladies, and flat-footed policemen. His editorial judgment was always soundest at that level. He never finally rid himself of an immature delight in scraps of useless information, on which *Tit-Bits* flourished.

A feature called *Curiosities* that ran through *The Strand* for many years was probably a legacy of his editorial activity. Its obsession with freaks and other aberrations of nature; for example, 'queer-shaped potatoes'; the room in the Ipswich home of Whitfield King, the well-known East Anglian stamp dealer, papered entirely with postage stamps valued at

£699 16s 9d; 'remarkable wedding cakes'; and feats of the tedious is-this-a-record kind, were in direct descent from the runaway train of long before. *Curiosities* was not always a compliment to the general intelligence level of readers of *The Strand* and there was perhaps significance in its relegation to the back pages.

The larger and longer view was taken in articles suggesting that flying and broadcasting would soon be removed from the scale of imponderables into the realm of the probable. Professor Langley, of the Smithsonian Institute, Washington, gave *The Strand* a full account of his experiments with a large model flying machine (which he called an aerodrome) powered by a steam engine. 'It has actually flown for considerable distances and thus, at last, solved the puzzle of aerial flight.'

If that seemed an extravagant claim, the professor could fairly insist that he had advanced men's knowledge of aerodynamics and laid down a mathematical runway for further experimental work. His pioneering labours went largely unacknowledged by those who benefited by them. He wrote in *The Strand*: 'For the next stage it is probable that the world may look to others. The world would indeed be supine if it does not realise that a new possibility has come to it and that the great universal highway overhead is now soon to be opened.'

Broadcasting was envisaged in the magazine in 1898 by Arthur Mee, subsequently editor of *The Children's Encyclopedia*, who reported that a system of telephony was operating in Budapest by which subscribers could be switched on to concerts and news services. He foresaw an expansion of the system 'conveying business and pleasure into thousands of homes. All that is necessary is a central office from which the whole of London—if not the whole of England—might be supplied with a constant flow of news and pleasure all day long'.

He speculated on the possibility of listeners hearing a Budget speech direct from the lips of a Chancellor of the Exchequer and of Stock Exchange transactions being conducted as a result of facilities provided by the system. 'Who dare to say that in twenty years the electric miracle will not bring all the corners of the earth to our own fireside?'

Another kind of speculation was put before readers in an unpublished article by General Gordon, in which *The Strand* secured the first publication rights. It was headed: *The Site of the Garden of Eden*, assigned by Gordon to Praslin, one of the smaller islands of the Seychelles group. A full descriptive account was reinforced by the general's own sketch maps. The article, said an editorial introduction, was 'written with deep religious feeling'.

By then assuming editorial control, Greenhough Smith grew in stature with it. He carried himself as if bound by a Hippocratic oath of his profession, until in time he qualified for admission to the small circle of those aristocrats of journalism, the great editors. As with most of them, it was a circumscribed greatness. He might not have expanded and flourished elsewhere.

He was a Cambridge man (St John's), whose entry in *Who's Who* gave no date of birth and stated that he was the 'son of Alfred Smith, engineer'. He was born at Stroud, Gloucestershire, in 1855. In his early years he was a private tutor. He wrote one or two novels that drew him into the publishing orbit.

Tall, lean, sandy-moustached, with freckles to match on a pallid expressionless face, he surveyed the world with kindly scrutineering eyes through rimless *pince-nez*. His distrust of emotion gave an impression of a temperament that did not fully warrant the nickname by which he was known to his fellow clubmen, 'Calamity' Smith. It may never have been spoken in his hearing, for his friends knew better than to take a liberty with him.

'How about a game of billiards?' he was good-naturedly asked by a famous musical comedy actor, Harry Welchman. There was an awkward pause. 'You refuse?' Welchman inquired. Greenhough Smith replied in his quietest tone: 'I don't refuse to play billiards. I refuse to be genial.'

He married a girl much younger than himself, 'straight from the nursery', in the words of Mrs C. N. Williamson, who wrote stories for *The Strand* and who knew them both. The young wife became a champion skater, representing England in international events. Greenhough Smith was a poker player of the first class. He would probably have preferred to go on record as the authority on French poetry that he certainly was.

He lived in a flat in what was then London's highest private building, Queen Anne's Mansions, S.W. Every day, for most of forty years, he walked into St James's Park, across the bridge, into the Mall and through Admiralty Arch, up to Southampton Street, to resume his place in one of the most coveted of editorial chairs.

After seeing him at work at his desk in shirtsleeves on a summer's day, surrounded by the trailing galley proofs of articles and stories, a colleague said: 'You could tell that he loved the job. You also knew that he would have resigned rather than admit it.'

Wary of originality, he was prepared to encourage it but not at the expense of readability or of the reputation of the magazine. If doubt entered his head about a particular story or article, he was most likely to reject it rather than take a chance of its succeeding with the readers. He believed in prompt decisions, on the ground that it was not fair to writers to keep them waiting. New contributors to *The Strand* were often surprised, not to say delighted, by the speed with which their cheques arrived. Payment on acceptance was a Newnes rule, much fairer than the payment on publication that prevailed in other publishing houses.

Greenhough Smith expected honesty from his short story writers. 'First impression,' he would insist, 'are important. As you begin, so you must go on,' meaning that there should be consistency of character and narrative. He would cite as an example of the wrong method *The Three Musketeers*, in which the opening episode of the missing documents has no later relevance. He required his contributors to share his sense of responsibility to the public.

For many years over coffee at the Savage Club, then in Adelphi Terrace, at his favourite table overlooking the river, he was joined in a word-making card game called Spelka (anticipating the far better known Lexicon), by Eille Norwood, whom many thought the best screen impersonator of Sherlock Holmes, R. D. Blumenfeld, editor of the *Daily Express*, and

Paul Verrall, a leading London orthopaedic surgeon. Sitting there, chain-smoking cigarettes in a long holder resting in the V of his tapering thin fingers, he was respectfully pointed out to guests less often by name than as 'the editor of *The Strand Magazine*'.

SEVEN

Dawn of a New Century

I

The nation stayed up till midnight by home fires, in churches and chapels, on cathedral steps, in village halls, in public squares. Beacons were ready for the kindling flame on all the highest hilltops, from the South Downs to the Mendips and on up to the Pennines and the Border beyond. All over the land, bellringers stood by their ropes, the coloured salleys resting in their hands, waiting.

It was December 31, 1899. Was it really the end of the nineteenth century? There were public and private doubts. Conan Doyle maintained that it was. Greenhough Smith said that it was not. 'I thought, and still think, that the end of the century was on December 31, 1900.'

In Westminster Abbey, a future Bishop of Oxford, Charles Gore, ascended the pulpit to express disappointment at the manner of the ending of the nineteenth century, and 'a buoyant, trustful hope for great things in the twentieth'. Described in the *Daily Mail* as 'leaning down over the sides of the pulpit and flinging his words clear and strong down the aisles', he took it as an occasion to declare: 'Our present-day literature is singularly without inspiration. There is no Carlyle to whom all men naturally turn to find some answer to their chaotic yearnings; there is no Tennyson to put into exquisite and melodious words the feelings of the educated. There is no prophet for the people.'

At St Paul's, Canon Mason from Canterbury preached to a vast congregation from the text: *I am Alpha and Omega; the beginning and the end*, and reminded his hearers of time's irrevocable perspectives. 'It is curious to think that to those born in the new century Wellington will be as distant as

Marlborough is to us, and Darwin will seem as Newton to the present generation; while Wordsworth, Tennyson, and Browning, whom we regard as the great poets of our time, will be as shadowy and remote as Pope and Gray.'

Half an hour later, the doom of the old century was sounded by the first throbbing stroke of the midnight chime. Beacons blazed, steeples trembled, crowds cheered. 'An annihilating roar of jubilation' spread across the world.

The Strand Magazine had sent out an inquirer with the question: What will be the greatest achievements of science in the new century? Discussing the uncertainties of prediction, Sir William Preece, chief engineer of the General Post Office and an active promoter of modern communications, including wireless telegraphy, told the *Strand* interrogator: 'We all ridiculed the telephone when it was first announced to the world. I went over to New York in 1877 with the intention of exposing the fraud. Graham Bell, the inventor, convinced me after five minutes' conversation.'

He could not see wireless telegraphy developing beyond its uses for 'marine and military purposes'. He expected that there would be a future for wireless telephony, 'chiefly as a means of communication between ships at sea or between islands'. No one, not even Marconi, he said, had 'the clue to messages through space over an indefinite distance'.

Pertaining to 'the possibility of twentieth-century man flying through the air', Preece insisted: 'If we are to have a real flying machine it must be based on some entirely new principle, at present altogether beyond our conception.' He thought that 'we can have no such hope'. No more than eight years later, his judgment was demolished by the Wright brothers.

Professor Sir William Crookes, F.R.S., the discoverer of a new element called thallium, had been reading H. G. Wells's story, *When the Sleeper Wakes*. 'I found that every one of the things imagined by the author to have taken place was merely a further extension of something which we have already.' Crookes did not doubt that the flying machine would be perfected in the new century. 'It is now, I believe, only a matter of money.'

He foresaw a great extension of 'twopenny tubes', and of the telephone service. 'Every house in London will be connected.' The phonograph (as the gramophone was then called) would be a source of common household entertainment. He suggested as a practical possibility that at some future time London might be roofed in with glass. He believed that great benefits would flow from the eternal energy of radium.

The inventor of the electric light bulb, Sir Joseph Swan, F.R.S., did not accept the notion that electrical appliances would be of labour-saving use in the home. 'I don't think it likely that electricity will be found advantageous for, say, cleaning the windows and scrubbing the floors, as imaginative writers have suggested, although a few people may choose to employ it as an exquisite way of having such things done.' Nor did he think it probable that electricity would supersede gas as an illuminant.

Looking beyond his science of chemistry, Sir Henry Roscoe, sometime President of the British Association, forecast 'the harnessing of many Niagaras as a source of future power. A former President of the Royal College of Surgeons thought that the limit of the uses of anaesthetics and antiseptics had been reached, that cancer and tuberculosis would be vanquished, along with the plague in India and malaria everywhere. He foresaw great advances in bacteriology, especially in the cultivation of 'friendly bacteria'.

The director of the Solar Physics Laboratory, Sir Norman Lockyer, posed the likelihood that the most important contributions to twentieth-century astronomical science would come from the United States, 'which now has more observers and better instruments than either England or Germany'. He looked forward to the chemical classification of the stars; the completion of a photographic chart of the heavens; the substitution of photography for the observations of individuals in recording 'transits' of stars; and to more knowledge of the practical effects of sunspots on human life.

In the next two years astronomical photography was to record 'a stupendous revelation', the birth and death of the *New Star of the New Century*, which burst upon the sight of men on February 22, 1901. The pictures published in

The Strand were remarkable. Science was beginning to communicate with the people in a way that had never before been possible.

Sir John Wolfe Barry, the engineer of the Tower Bridge—'that terrible mixture of medievalism and machinery'[1]—foresaw the need to provide for 'an enormously increased and ever-increasing traffic in the streets'. One of his proposals for dealing with it was 'overhead moving platforms'. A Channel tunnel, he assured *The Strand*, was a practical possibility. He thought that there was a case for an Irish Channel tunnel too.

Parliament's attitude to the Tunnel was recorded for *The Strand* by Sir Henry Lucy in *From Behind the Speaker's Chair*. Mr Gladstone was in favour and had supported it 'by many luminous speeches'. Lord Randolph Churchill and Mr Joseph Chamberlain were against it. As President of the Board of Trade, Chamberlain halted work on the project.

Its principal promoter in the House, Sir Edward Watkin, who had toiled long and wearisomely in the cause, vowed that if the work was permanently stopped, he would 'erect on the site at the British end a pillar of stone lofty enough to be seen by ships passing up and down the great waterway'. On it he would have inscribed: *This Work was Stopped by Joseph Chamberlain of Birmingham*.

To the stock argument that in case of war with France 'the approach to our island home would be a source of danger', Watkin demonstrated to Parliament 'how by an electric button pressed in a room in London the British end of the tunnel could be blown up', to which Lucy appended the recollection: 'This greatly tickled Lord Randolph's fancy.'

Like most of their kind, the scientists who were interviewed for *The Strand* mistrusted public exercise of their imaginations. They gave no hint of convulsions to come in scientific thought, no glimpse of the terrifying logic of Einstein and Rutherford. If they were not crazily certain of the future, they left the readers of *The Strand* in little doubt of their belief that progress in science as in all else could only be ensured by the exercise of the Victorian disciplines.

[1] H. G. Wells.

2

Heavy with virtue, in its sumptuous advertising at the front and back, as in the judiciously chosen editorial contents between, averaging 62,000 words of good reading every month, *The Strand* entered the new age as a powerful cultural determinant. If in retrospect it is seen as another demonstration of the middle-class trading code of life, hallowed by beneficent intentions, there can be no doubting the warmth of the appreciation that awaited its monthly appearance wherever the English race had settled. A traveller leaving Waterloo by boat train for Southampton noted that 'every other person on the train had a copy'. Arriving at Cape Town, he saw that a pile of copies of the magazine on the railway bookstall was 'diminishing with rapidity'.

Conan Doyle wrote to Greenhough Smith after returning from the Continent: 'Foreigners used to recognise the English by their check suits. I think they will soon learn to do it by their *Strand Magazines*. Everybody on the Channel boat, except the man at the wheel, was clutching one.'

For the exiles in many lands the monthly arrival of *The Strand* was reassurance of abiding values at a stage in history when, for example, a *Daily Mail* leading article uttered the warning that England was 'entering stormy seas and the time may be near when we shall have to fight in truth for our life'.[1]

A shadow from the ominous future was thrown across the pages by an article on the 26th Middlesex Cyclists' Regiment, shown in photographs parading with tricycles as mobile gun mountings. For most readers it was a first sign of mechanisation as a new departure in military thinking. As if to point an incredible contrast, in another article the Charge of the Light Brigade was described by a Hussar who took part in it.

The uses of pigeons as 'messengers of war' were discussed by A. H. Osman, for whom destiny had reserved the role of officer commanding pigeons in the great war to come. He deemed it important that readers of *The Strand* should know that 'in France no foreigner is allowed to keep racing pigeons'. A parliamentary watchdog, Logan, M.P., was invoked for the

[1] December 31, 1900.

opinion: 'Instead of bothering about a pigeon post for use when an army has landed, we had better make perfectly sure that no invading army shall ever land.' Readers of *The Strand* could take heart from noting that while the Middlesex Cyclists' Regiment might be inhibited from dare-devilry by their tricycles, they looked a resolute body of men.

Apparently *The Strand*, which appeared to have an editorial bias in favour of the timeless as against the timely, could not avoid the war theme when, apart from the conflict in South Africa, the beating of German military drums was becoming louder on the air. An illustrated article entitled *Precipice-Riding In The Continental Armies* particularly stressed the training of German army horses at 'The Sand' outside Bonn. 'A sharp headlong declivity of loose earth runs down from a field to an open common for a distance of from 70ft. or 80ft. and the soldiers are taken down it *at a gallop*!'

No moral was drawn, no suggestion made of any sinister intent. Readers, left with the implication that there was more in those peculiar evolutions than met the eye, experienced the shiver of the nerves that so many German activities excited from the turn of the century onwards.

Already Rider Haggard, not long since sprung to fame as the author of *She*, had expressed to a *Strand* interviewer a dismay that was to become in our later time a national malaise. He was speaking of his experiences as an official observer of the British capitulation after Majuba. 'I was so overcome with the disgrace of the situation that I abandoned South Africa. I felt that I could no longer live there as an Englishman.' Seeing Haggard at the private view of the Royal Academy, Beckles Willson, a frequent contributor to the magazine, wrote in his diary: 'Physically, he is like a respectable farmer. The day of Bulwer, Ainsworth and Dickens, who looked like novelists, is over.'

Despite Rider Haggard's misgivings, the bugle note of Empire was confidently sounded by Rudyard Kipling, making his first bow in *The Strand* with a short story called *The Lost Legion*. He had recently and not altogether percipiently been depicted in the magazine as a typical member of the London Press Club by a new caricaturist who signed his work H. Maxwell Beerbohm.

3

One has an impression of the decorum of the magazine being as solid and as polished as the mahogany in Sir George Newnes's office. In the matter of the taste, the deference to readers was complete. There was much earnest 'vetting' of text, pictures, advertisements. The same strict standards were upheld in American opposite numbers of *The Strand*.

At *Scribner's* a story was long current that when in the early 1900s the magazine published an article on contemporary French art, and used a nude as one of the illustrations, an important advertiser wrote complaining that, on seeing it, his wife 'uttered a low cry and ran from the room'. From then on, any illustration thought likely to provoke a similar reaction was known in *Scribner's* office as a 'low cry' picture.

Emphasis on the proprieties was part of the rigid social context and was necessarily reflected in the editorial policy of the magazine. It did not mean for *The Strand*, as it did for some magazines then, and many more since, a policy of seducing readers from the harsh realities, of exploiting romantic love and glamourising human relationships in general.

The Strand was prepared to send its writers into 'a district teeming with the poor' to collect facts for an article about the Children's Hospital in Great Ormond Street, or to Whitechapel for information about the life of its polyglot population. A local photographer explained that 'he had to be careful not to take a certain type of Jewish feature in profile, for the foreign Jew, once he has been acclimatised, does not like to look "sheeny" '. As for 'the descendants of Ham—euphemistically classed under the generic term of "gentlemen of colour"—they were fearful lest their features should come out too dark'. Clearly, integration is not the new problem that many suppose it to be.

An investigation of the conditions of child labour in the big cities produced vivid material for the notebooks of social historians. 'Children find an endless variety of ways of earning a living in the streets. There are the boot-black boys, who form a useful portion of the community; newspaper boys, of whom the better sort are careful little capitalists, with an immense fund of intelligence and commercial instinct; "job chaps" who hang about railway stations on the chance of earning a few pence by carrying bags; flower-girls, match-girls, crossing-sweepers, who can make a fair living if they are industrious; and lastly—although this enumeration by no means exhausts the lists—street prodigies, such as pavement painters and musicians. All Londoners must be familiar with the figure of little Master Sorine, who sits perched up on a high stool diligently painting away at a marine-scape in highly coloured chalks. This clever little artist of eleven is the principal support of his parents.'

Some of the levels of drudgery revealed by the article are unthinkable today. 'Unfortunate is the lot of some of the little girl workers who assist their mothers at home in tailoring, button-making, and dolls' clothes-making. The united work of mother and child yields only a wretched pittance, and, carried on as it is in a room where sleeping, eating, and living go on, is, of all forms of labour, the saddest and most unhealthy. Meals consist of bread and tea, and work is prolonged till midnight by the light of one candle, with the consequence that the children are prematurely aged and diseased,' the writer finally observing: 'This is the most painful kind of child labour that I have come across, and would be unbearable if it were not ennobled by the touching affection that almost invariably exists between the worn-out mother and her old-woman-wise little daughter.'

The moralising tailpiece was typical. There had to be assurance of virtue persisting with dandelion brightness in basements where the light of day was only dimly seen and privation was the common lot. There was no criticism of the society in which that form of degradation could flourish. Information was gathered and collated with gloved hands and put before the readers with a genteel regard for their susceptibilities.

There was in all this an observable grace that ran through many years of the magazine's existence, an unproclaimed good form that buttressed its dignity and authority. It was a matter not of ignoring social evils but of disdaining to 'cash in' on them in the spirit of the muck-raking journalism that by then was sending up even respectable circulations across the Atlantic.

An unusual example of austere comment was to be found in an article on the county courts, in which the anonymous writer maintained that 'it is notorious that many of the judges are totally unfit for even the decent performance of their work. Some are worn-out old men who are quite incapacitated by deafness and other infirmities, to say nothing of ignorance, stupidity, and querulousness, and their retention on the Bench constitutes a great evil to suitors as well as a public scandal'. One searches through many volumes without finding a repetition of that tone, which perhaps at the time was taken as complying with the well-established Newnes formula for editors: Information as entertainment.

4

The quickening pace is manifest in the first *Strand* volume of the twentieth century, that for January-June 1900. Newnes's dream of a picture on every page was all but realised, aided by the camera which was opening new windows on the world in every issue. There is no picture of a motorcar in the 720 pages of that volume, though Sir George Newnes was one of the first car owners and one of the first substantial investors in internal combustion transport.

The motorcar was still an object of suspicious doubt among many people who detested the noise, oil, and dust inseparable from it. Maeterlinck, the Belgian philosopher poet, was writing about it as if it were a mystical entity, with 'its trembler-blade, sparking plugs, and many other organs of which I scarcely dare let myself speak'.

Yet *The Strand* was giving its readers lavishly illustrated articles on such modern developments as skyscraper building, bridge building, and lighthouse building, showing its alertness to the imminence of dramatically accelerated change. Readers were informed in the accents of the marvellous that 'Chicago is now within eight days' comfortable journey from London'.

The appointment of Grant Allen (1848–1899) as a regular contributor on scientific topics was another editorial decision in tune with the times. After Oxford and preparatory school-mastering, he became sufficiently distinguished in life and letters to warrant a handsome entry in the *Dictionary of National Biography*. When some of his learned friends, who included Charles Darwin, T. H. Huxley, Herbert Spencer and Alfred Russel Wallace, expressed pained surprise that he had written a serial story for *Tit-Bits*, he answered that the thousand pounds he was paid for it saved him from the 'slow starvation' that faced him as a writer on science for the monthly reviews. He was a semi-permanent invalid who subsisted chiefly on oysters and Benger's Food.

Conan Doyle said that as an interpreter of science to the general reading public Allen 'stood alone'. He was the first writer to convey the meaning of the Darwinian theory to the understanding of the multitude. His objective view of the human situation, set out in such books as his *Evolution of the Idea of God*, caused him to be mistrusted by conventionally-minded persons. 'Remember, John,' a wife returning a call with her husband was heard to say on Allen's doorstep, 'if he openly blasphemes, we leave the room.'

Conan Doyle, who went to see him in his last illness, has left a poignant impression of the experience: 'I can see him now, his knees drawn up to ease internal pain, and his long thin nose and reddish-grey goatee protruding over the sheet, while he croaked out: "Byzantine art, my dear Doyle, was of three periods, the middle one roughly coinciding with the actual fall of the Roman Empire. The characteristics of the first period——" and so on, until he would give a cry, clasp his hands across his stomach, and wait till the pain had passed before resuming his lecture.'[1]

A literary weekly drew attention to two wills published in the *Daily Chronicle* one day towards the end of 1899: Charles Grant Blairfindie Allen, author, died October 25, aged 51: £6455 gross, net personalty £3500. Francis Hudson, cheesemonger, died October 26, aged 63: £275,810 gross, net personalty £190,086.

Photographs illustrating an article on ballooning over London may have been the first published examples of the aerial

[1] Sir Arthur Conan Doyle: *Memories and Adventures* (1924).

use of the camera, which was becoming the most fascinating toy of the age. The results were novel rather than instructive. They could have passed off as specimens of the bacteriological studies from which the ex-President of the Royal College of Surgeons expected such great things.

The New Photography had already told of the wonders of Röntgen's X-ray discoveries, and the accompanying pictures of the skeletal formations of animals and, even more exciting, those showing the bones of the human hand, a shot embedded in a rabbit's foot, and the nails in a boot, indicated startling new possiblities of scientific exploration. *Building A Giant Telescope* was a symptom of the still more daring curiosity that would animate science in the next fifty years.

Contrasting with the signs and portents, the story illustrations in *The Strand* continued to confirm the old and familiar. Maids in caps and aprons opened front doors to admit frock-coated men who handed in their silk hats as they advanced genuflectingly towards ladies with chignons and lorgnettes. Basement servitude was unrelieved. Town pavements were studded with the iron lids of coal holes. 'Tradesmen's Entrance' was a mark of still implacable class patronage. There was a strong smell of gas, the greatest public utility of the time.

EIGHT

W. W. Jacobs and some others

I

While posing as a family magazine, *The Strand* primarily appealed to men: no anomaly, seeing that paterfamilias was still all powerful in the domestic circle. Bret Harte, Dick Donovan, George Manville Fenn, W. Clark Russell, and other swashbucklers with the pen did not seek the suffrages of women readers. Neither did Conan Doyle and those who immediately followed him in the pages of *The Strand*: W. W. Jacobs, Rudyard Kipling, H. G. Wells, E. W. Hornung, A. E. W. Mason.

Women's fiction needs at that time were provided for by Mrs L. T. Meade, 'Rita' (Mrs Humphreys), Winifred Graham, Mrs Baillie Reynolds, Mrs C. N. Williamson, Coralie Stanton. Their work was valued at an average of five guineas a thousand words. Some issues went to press with no story or article of compelling interest to women.

A series of half-tone portraits of 'society beauties', entwined in printers' 'flowers' and arabesques, may have been intended to soften the ponderous masculine overtones. When an article headed simply *Babies* (cradle customs of the world) was followed by another entitled *The Magic of Hairdressing*, the effect was of a startling editorial *volte-face*.

The hairdressing article, long and heavy with historical allusions, was illustrated by photographs of Decima Moore, a picture postcard favourite in her day, modelling a range of exotic hair styles. Some time in the late '30s, I met at a cocktail party a dainty little silver-haired old lady in whose face there lingered the oval serenity of *The Strand Magazine* illustrations of long ago. 'I'm Decima Moore,' she announced in a patrician voice and her diamond monogram clasp sparkled as a proof of it. 'I married old Guggisberg, you know,'[1] as if fate, rather than destiny, had decreed that denouement of her success on the stage.

For a fleeting moment the footlights glowed again, the violin bows cast their busy shadows on the great brocaded curtain, and echoes of forgotten Gilbert and Sullivan numbers rose like champagne bubbles from the gay Edwardian past.

2

The name E. Nesbit, recurring in the indexes of those old volumes, suggests a similar if less drastic change in policy. Readers believed that E. Nesbit was a man. So convinced were they that when she dedicated a book to her husband some took it as a practical joke and refused to accept it as revealed truth. There were letters of hers in the office files, sent from her home, Well Hall, Eltham, Kent. They were written on narrow docket-like slips of paper in a clear attractive hand. Her E (for Edith) was rotund with personality.

She was recalled by Havelock Ellis and doubtless by others as a woman of 'radiant vitality'. She and her first husband, Hubert Bland, one-time bank clerk, afterwards a journalist, were ardent Fabians from the first meeting of the Society, which had sprung directly from a 'crackpot' group called the Fellowship of New Life. Edward Pease, secretary of the Fabian Society, spoke of her as 'most vivacious and attractive'. She has been described in print as 'an exceptionally handsome, tall, slender young woman, with a figure at once strong, graceful, and supple; eyes dark but bright and very watchful, beautiful eyebrows, and a fine broad forehead half covered by a fringe of naturally curly brown hair'.[2] Her glance and head movements were darting and bird-like.

Among her friends and close acquaintances were Shaw (with whom she briefly fell in love), William Morris, Bradlaugh, Annie Besant, Edward Carpenter, Mrs Pankhurst, Ramsay MacDonald, Graham Wallas, Bertrand Russell, Wells.

[1] Major-General Sir Gordon Guggisberg, K.C.M.G., D.S.O., sometime C.-in-C. Gold Coast.
[2] From *E. Nesbit, A Biography*, by Doris Langley Moore (Benn, 1933).

She dared convention by proclaiming herself a Socialist; dared it again by refusing to wear corsets and, yet again, by smoking cigarettes in public, one of the first Englishwomen of the 1880s to do so.

Her zeal for social justice, toughened by semi-poverty in her early married years, was wholly sincere. It did not preclude her from rising above the subjective view. She discussed some of her fellow Fabians in a letter. 'Mr V—writes plays— interested in social questions and dried fruits. Mr U—has a passion for being thought *deep* and *mystical*, which leads him to be rather aggravating at times.'[1] Not every Fabian understood, and some could not forgive, the tolerance she showed towards her husband's infidelities. They brought her much unhappiness and yet did not wreck the marriage. When she discovered that he had fathered a child elsewhere, she called on the mother to offer sympathy and help. She wrote a possibly relevant novel, *The Incomplete Amorist*.

She was a poet who received distinguished encouragement; from Swinburne, for instance, and the Rossettis. As a novelist, she tended to be opinionated, limiting her appeal. Her tales for the young supplied some of the best remembered pleasures of the childhood of two generations: *The Bastables, The Would-be-Goods, The House of Arden, Story of the Treasure Seekers, The Wonderful Garden, The Railway Children.*[2] She has no more devoted admirer than Noel Coward who, at school, saved his pocket money to buy back numbers of *The Strand Magazine* containing her stories: *The Psammead, The Phoenix and the Carpet, The Amulet.* Analytical minds have claimed to find in certain of his stage characters prototype affinities with Oswald Bastable.

A more immediately contemporary voice was raised in salute to her in 1965 when an American novelist and critic, Gore Vidal, told the *Sunday Times*: 'Nothing could be more wrong than to regard her as a dated relic of nineteenth-century kiddies' whimsy. She was rigorously honest in a proper documentary way about how children and adults lived.

[1] Moore, op. cit.
[2] 'Without a doubt, they are immensely good'—J. B. Priestley, in *The Bookman*, 1924.

She was one of the few writers who realised that children, like Jews and Negroes, are a persecuted minority.' He asked: 'Has anyone realised that *The Railway Children* is in part a fictional recreation, from the child's point of view, of the Dreyfus case?'

I pose a less recondite question. Did *The Railway Children* (still in print, still widely read, televised by the B.B.C.) have its genesis, like *Tit-Bits* and all that, in the runaway train newspaper story of 1881? In the 1870s, E. Nesbit lived at Halstead, near Knockholt, Kent. She spent her early girlhood there. It was from Halstead station that the train started on its headlong course towards London with the stationmaster's children as its only passengers.

The brief report seen by George Newnes in the Manchester paper was almost certainly supplied by a news agency, which meant that it also appeared in other newspapers, north and south. Its connection with Halstead would have been registered firmly in the mind of E. Nesbit, assuming that she read it or heard about it. One's fancy clings obstinately to the likelihood that she did so, to the delight of young hearts everywhere. The book that it may have suggested was written much later. Episodes in it bear the marks of derivative influence. It was known that E. Nesbit often went back to Halstead in the years between to walk in woods and fields where she had found happiness as a girl.

Seventeen of her books are still in print. Six have lately been reprinted by Penguin. Foreign rights in her work are a subject of frequent transactions. The royalties yield a steady four-figure income.

3

If we look through the volumes of *The Strand* for the first decade of the 1900s we see that a wind of change had blown down Southampton Street, taking with it much of the Victorian stuffiness, particularly from the art side of the magazine. Pages are tidier and less often disfigured by drawings with dramatic heavy-wash backgrounds. There are many photographs, giving a sense of topicality that is sometimes more apparent than real.

The art editor had evidently issued an edict: Let there be more light, banning the idiosyncratic illustrators who went in for 'spatter work', or devotees of the fussy effects obtained with the aid of a minute milled wheel propelled by a pen-holder. Drawings were squared off in bold framing lines; and there seems to have been a keener precision in the choice of subjects illustrated. The total result was a rejuvenated make-up that even now retains some of that pristine freshness.

There was a reversal of policy in the fiction department. Serial stories, in Newnes's original planning of the magazine discounted as being suited only to the *Tit-Bits* type of periodical, were admitted and quickly proved that the monthly interval was no bar to the readers' enjoyment of F. Anstey's *Brass Bottle*, Conan Doyle's *The Hound of the Baskervilles*, H. G. Wells's *First Men in the Moon*, W. W. Jacobs's *A Master of Craft*, Rudyard Kipling's *Puck of Pook's Hill*. *The Hound of the Baskervilles*, allegedly an early adventure of Sherlock Holmes, put 30,000 copies on to *The Strand* circulation.

The Strand was paying the highest prices (and in doing so helping to give solidity to the new profession of literary agent) for its fiction; for example, for instalments of *The Hound of the Baskervilles* Conan Doyle received not less than £480 and as much as £620, according to the length. From the mid-90s, he never had less than £100 a thousand words from *The Strand*.

The counting house calculated to the nearest shilling the amounts due to authors paid at a fixed rate per thousand words. For *The Grey Parrot* W. W. Jacobs received £63 13s 4d and for *The Madness of Mr Lister*, £86 13s 4d. For his short story, *Mr Brasher's Treasure*, H. G. Wells was paid £83 6s 4d. His *The Truth About Pyecraft* commanded the round sum of £125.

In after years, Wells laid a complaint against the popular magazines for 'deadening the conception of what a short story might be'. True, the *coterie* magazines were encouraging a high standard of short story writing; too high for a wide reading audience. 'We want stories—stories, not dialect sketches, not washed-out studies of effete human nature, not weak tales of sickly sentimentality, not "pretty" writing. We want fiction in which there is a story, a force, a tale that means something—in short, a story. Good writing is common . . . good stories are rare.'

The formula, enunciated by Munsey, the American magazine publisher, would have been endorsed by Greenhough Smith, who knew that his public, aggregating two and perhaps three millions, preferred action to introspection, adventure to analysis, doing to thinking, appreciation to depreciation.

When, long after, I occupied the editorial chair, I wrote in my notebooks that 'however irresponsible those early short-story writers of ours may seem to our war-tried, more mature, generations, they were at least untainted by the modern relish for moral renunciation. They were not egotistically oppressed by the indifference of the universe. They did not fashion their plots out of man's bewilderments and fears, nor did they have any part in the brutal disillusioning process to which many of the new writers put their gifts. Case-history writing did not interest them and they would have despised the current obsession with violence that reduces authorship to the level of a criminal occupation'.

4

The Strand enabled W. W. Jacobs (1863–1943) to retire from his post in the Savings Bank Department of the General Post Office in 1899 to produce those tales of waterside characters that appear and reappear in *The Skipper's Wooing, Odd Craft, Many Cargoes, The Lady of the Barge, Night Watches,* and *At Sunwich Port.* They are minor rogues, cheats, liars, deceivers, artful opportunists in a comic tradition that makes even their crudest behaviour amusing.

'It was a wet, dreary night in that cheerless part of the great metropolis known as Wapping . . . ' It is irresistible incitement, however rascally the company. Jacobs has us by the ear and there is no ducking away from his hold. It should be added that our sympathies are further enlisted by the imaginative skill of *The Strand Magazine* illustrations by Will

Owen. His renderings of Bob Pretty, Sam Small, Ginger Dick, Henry Walker, Peter Russet, may have been as indispensable to Jacobs's success as Sidney Paget was to Conan Doyle's.

Before *The Strand* brought him fame, Jacobs had made no public mark, although he had written for various publications, *Chambers' Journal* and *The Idler* among them. Newnes bought two stories from him for *The Million*. That paper's fate was Jacobs's fortune. Greenhough Smith liked the stories and thenceforward the door of *The Strand Magazine* stood invitingly open to him. The magazine printed all his future work. It was a successful arrangement for both sides. Jacobs's work was equally popular with readers of the American edition of *The Strand*.

He was born at Wapping, the son of the manager of the South Devon Wharf, and a member of a large family that knew hardship at the subsistence level. His great-grandfather was a skipper, in whose brig one of the royal Georges sailed to Flushing.

Slight in build, sharp of features, almost albino in colouring, which made him look younger than his years, he had the air of a nervously venturesome young curate. Shy in company, he spoke in a low-key tone, often delivering his opinions with Cockney furtiveness from the side of his mouth. In his more withdrawn moods he seemed to shrink physically.

The people for him were 'the herd', and he told Jerome K. Jerome, his literary godfather: 'I am not sure that I do want the greatest happiness for the greatest number.' When Jerome told him that under Socialism his simple needs would be assured, Jacobs snapped back with an impatience that stirs echoes in the corridors of Welfare State officialdom: 'I don't want things to be assured to me. I'd hate a lot of clever people fussing about, making me happy and doing me good. Damn their eyes!'

He married Agnes Eleanor Williams, an accountant's daughter, an attractive and spirited young woman twenty years younger than himself, who 'got ideas' and pursued a political line at variance with his inflexible Conservatism. She joined the suffragettes, broke windows, went to prison.

Later in his life, Jacobs wrote privately from his home at

Beechcroft, Berkhamsted, to the editor of the *Daily Mail*, begging that a letter of hers should not be printed. 'It is awkward for me, as people foolishly presume that I share her views. Hers are those of the *Daily Herald*, Lenin & Co. Mine are Conservative. Hotly opposed to my views, my wife is quite ready to use my name to further her own ends. Alas, it is an unscrupulous sex!' The 'bossy' type of female was a character in many of his stories.

Alec Waugh, who was their son-in-law for a brief unhappy period (described with sensitive feeling in *The Early Years of Alec Waugh*),[1] disclosed that she was the heroine of H. G. Wells's novel, *The Wife of Sir Isaac Harman*. The marriage became one of the unnumbered sorry spectacles of the domestic arena. Whether and how it affected Jacobs's performance as a writer are unanswered questions. His productive career was contained in no more than fifteen of his eighty years. He was apparently not impelled to write a major work. Ambition and he were strangers.

He was a tortuously slow writer who 'pottered about' endlessly, sometimes for a whole morning, while trying to frame a sentence. There was a legend at *The Strand* that writing a story of four or five thousand words was as exhausting to him as an athletic feat and that there was usually a sequel of rest away from home. He was a master of understatement and the loaded hint; no writer used both more pointedly. He did not speak for his characters; he let them speak for themselves in their own idiom. His stories are anecdotes fine-spun to their tensile limits by a skill that assigned place and value to every word.

'Sam's Boy', in *Light Freights*, remains one of the most genuinely amusing forays in the realm of humorous writing The stratagems of the homeless boy who, after watching a mongrel dog force itself on a reluctant stranger, applies the same technique to an artless sailor, is a typically ingenious idea of Jacobs's, triumphantly carried out.

The quiet humour that was his most readily marketable gift had an obverse side, a certain pleasure in the uncanny, as shown in his celebrated short story, *The Monkey's Paw*,

1 Cassell, 1962.

which has been dramatised, televised, and many times reprinted. As one reads it the shadow of Edgar Allan Poe falls across the page, communicating an authentic shiver, if only faintly.

That it necessarily indicated a demonic element in Jacobs is anyone's guess. His few excursions into the macabre hardly suggest psychic stress and positively not poetic depth. Nor did he seem to have any deep sense of the world's woe, the inspiration of perhaps the greatest humorists.

Jacobs (Wapping and Rotherhithe) was the first of the 'local' writers who at the turn of the century were clearly identified by the reading public with a self-assigned domain: Israel Zangwill with London Jewry; Arthur Morrison with the East End slums; W. Pett Ridge and Edwin Pugh with the suburbs. Jacobs was the first, also, to break those bounds by allowing his fancy to wander inland to village life where it discovered a new rich vein of comedy, centred in the Cauliflower Inn at Claybury. He showed that rustic humour has precious little in common with the straw-sucking stage comic's version of it, that the wit of the four-ale bar could be as subtle, any day, as that heard over the wine-splashed table tops at the Café Royal.

Photographs of the leading *Strand Magazine* authors were displayed for many years on the walls of the editor's room, right up to my time. Jacobs, who seldom posed for the camera, was among them, aged about 30, hair neatly brushed and parted, white shirt cuffs showing; in appearance, the typical confidential clerk, in truth a natural humorist whose ear was as sharp as his eye and whose hold on the reading public requires that his books should still be kept in print. A comparison of him with another famous humorist of *The Strand* was made by a practised fellow professional, who considered that Jacobs was 'as much undervalued by the intelligentsia as Wodehouse, no funnier and less adroit and inventive, was over-praised by them'.[1] *The Fortnightly Review* had long before acclaimed Jacobs as 'perhaps the greatest master of the humorous short story known to any literature'.[2]

[1] J. B. Priestley: *Margin Released* (Heinemann, 1962).
[2] September 1908.

5

The Strand Magazine advertisements filled an average of a hundred pages a month, representing more than two hundred and fifty advertisers. They provided it with an envied revenue in its heyday. They indexed the domestic and social life of its readers with something like encyclopedic completeness. We become acquainted with the preferences, prejudices, habits, and conventions, of a wide section of society. A sociologist might discover more about the period from those back and front pages of *The Strand* than from the articles and stories between.

We follow the readers' evolving tastes in furnishings, fabrics, clothes, wallpapers, carpets, perambulators, kitchen ware. We see the holiday resorts bidding for their favours. We see the cars they coveted. We are reminded of the cosmetics they used and the patent medicines they took. Their secret dreams are laid bare to us; of putting inches on their height, banishing depilatory blemishes, growing luxuriant hair, qualifying for higher salaries by correspondence courses, acquiring *savoir faire*. We learn that their hobbies were fretwork, stamp collecting, pianola playing, and that roller skating and diabolo were among their more evanescent pastimes.

In the beginning, the advertisement typography was black and ugly, knowing no touch but the printer's. Layout was rough and ready, a Gothic jumble of goods and services: Fry's Pure Cocoa, Rowland's Macassar Oil Brilliantine, Vinolia Soap, Cuticura Soap, Pears' Soap, Dr Jaeger's Wool for Clothing, Southall's Sanitary Towels, Edwards' Desiccated Soup, 'Frame Food' Extract, The Bar-Lock Typewriter, Bird's Custard Powder, Carter's Little Liver Pills, Nestle's Food. A sign of the coming self-consciousness in advertising was given in a full page illustration of two sculptural figures in the classic mode, 'modelled by Mr J. A. Raemaker, R.A.' and inscribed 'What are the Wild Waves Saying? "Try Beecham's Pills".' It all accorded ill with the otherwise dignified presentation of the magazine.

Change impended in that department, as elsewhere, bringing

order and artistry to the overcrowded advertising pages and increasing their value tenfold. Every month the new advertising manager, Alfred Johnson, had to turn away would-be space buyers. As a selling medium, *The Strand* was at the top of its class for many years, a stimulus to higher production, better living standards, and the general prosperity.

"OLD SAM CREPT BACK 'OME LIKE A MAN IN A DREAM, WITH A BAG OF ORANGES HE DIDN'T WANT."

Sam Small, a famous W. W. Jacobs character, depicted by Will Owen.

NINE

'Illustrated Interviews'

I

'From the very first morning of his reign all the arteries of life in connection with the Crown felt the wholesome impulse of a fresh current.' *The Strand* political contributor, Sir Henry Lucy (1845–1924), made the accession of Edward VII an opportunity for regretting that the new monarch could no longer be the familiar figure in the parliamentary precincts that he had been as Prince of Wales. 'He comes into his new estate with an intimate personal knowledge of Parliamentary life possessed by none of his predecessors. For fully twenty-five years it has had a powerful fascination for him.'

We learn what some of us did not know, that during certain sessions the Prince was an almost nightly habitué of the Peers' Gallery in the House of Commons, an eyewitness of turbulent scenes made by Irish members and Bradlaugh's often execrated interventions in debate. Once, the Prince was forced to leave the gallery under the 'No strangers' rule.

He had gone down to the House to hear a debate. The member who rose to open it, Henry Chaplin, got no further than 'Mr Speaker, sir—'. A shrill back-bench voice called out: 'Mr Speaker, sir, I believe there are strangers in the House.' The Speaker, aware of the Prince's presence, did his best to ignore the challenge. The back-bencher would not desist. 'There was nothing for it,' Lucy reported for *The Strand*, 'but that the Prince of Wales, the representative of the German Emperor, the belted earls and barons in the Peers' Gallery, should file forth at the bidding of a gentleman who, when not assisting in the Government of the Empire, was engaged in the pork and bacon business in Belfast.'

Assuring readers that the Prince of Wales 'absolutely preserved the character of what Lord Granville happily designated the Cross Bench mind', the chronicler of Parliament for *The Strand* recalled an exception when the Deceased Wife's Sister Bill was before the House. 'The Prince of Wales frequently presented petitions in favour of the measure. When the motion for its second reading was divided upon, he invariably went out into the lobby in support of it, counting as an item in the number of peers who vote "content".' Lucy added in a tone of courtly deference: 'The Cross Bench in the Lords will never again be occupied by the illustrious person who is now King of Great Britain and Emperor of India.'

Sir Henry Lucy, from Crosby, Lancashire, was the son of a watchmaker's craftsman. After serving for seven years as a poorly paid clerk in the leather trade, he learnt shorthand as a hobby and by means of it secured a newspaper reporter's job at Shrewsbury. Graduating to Fleet Street, he was respected for his extreme and sometimes self-sacrificing loyalty to old colleagues. It inhibited him, for example, from accepting the editorship of *Punch*. He was editor of the Liberal *Daily News* for eighteen months, a post which Dickens had filled even more briefly. Tactful, dependable, indefatigable, he established himself as a political columnist (though that was not the term then) who had the regard of members of both Houses of Parliament.

From Behind The Speaker's Chair, his monthly article for *The Strand*, was suggested by Newnes over the dinner table. Lucy was not attracted because articles for *The Strand* had to be ready four weeks ahead of publication. It meant that he could not keep readers in touch with current sittings of the House. 'I proposed to get out of the difficulty by demanding what I thought would be a prohibitive price.' The *Strand* account books show that the 'prohibitive price' was £30 per article. He contributed the series regularly through every session of Parliament for ten years.

His success was in his ability to present Parliament as a continuing pageant in the life of the nation. He wrote neither as political analyst nor interpreter but as a journalist whose facile pen was governed by a strong sense of the historical past. He had Defoe's gift for seizing on vivid, relevant details.

A slip of his pen gratifyingly confirmed the quality of the magazine's readership. He had written that while the gift of a bishopric is in the hands of the Prime Minister, the nominee is chosen by the Bench of Bishops. He should have ascribed that function to the Dean and Chapter of the diocese concerned. 'Never has such a shower of correspondence descended upon my abashed head as followed that maladroit sentence. I seem to have heard from all the rectories and vicarages in England.'

His close scrutiny of the day to day proceedings in the House, and of the style, habits and foibles of its members, gained him a large following. Frequently his observations were more evocative of the personality of individuals than the wooden 'F.C.G.' cartoons that were meant to illustrate them.

'The House of Commons, watching with friendly interest the appearance on the Parliamentary scene of the son and heir of Lord Randolph Churchill, observes a curious mannerism in his speech.' Balfour's frequent interjection: 'Exactly!' was noted, and Campbell-Bannerman's change of name explained. 'He was elected as Henry Campbell and added the second patronymic in deference to a legacy.' When Sir Charles Dilke, in a speech on the Civil List, attacked Court extravagance, in which he was seconded, 'with almost hysterical vehemence' by Auberon Herbert, another member, Cavendish Bentinck, 'went behind the Speaker's chair and crowed thrice'.

Lucy had seen Disraeli in the full tide of his glory at a State opening of Parliament. It is not too much to say that interest in his appearance exceeded even that which surged round the coming of the Queen, 'holding aloft a sword whose scabbard was jewelled after a fashion his soul loved. He was conscious that all eyes were upon him—by his peers on the benches, by the Foreign Ministers, by the ladies in the gallery, by the Commons cooped in at the Bar. With measured pace, Dizzy moved along, looking neither to the right hand nor the left, his countenance as inscrutable as the carved stone-work in the desert'.

He saw Gladstone as Prime Minister, 'wearied to death'. There had been a stormy all-night sitting. 'As morning broke, he let his head fall back on the bench, closing his eyes and seeming to sleep, the worn face taking ten years of added life.'

A rather less than middle-size man with a cockatoo quiff and a bandmaster's moustache, Lucy carried himself with an air of well-being that was abundantly endorsed by the will revealed after his death in 1924. He never let his popularity among M.P.s cloud his opinions. He told readers of *The Strand* that the House of Lords was ordinarily a place of deadly dullness. 'The dumping-ground of the political world, it contains a considerable stratum of men who have either proved failures in the more active arena of the Commons or, after a more or less useful career, have reached a period of life when labour is but sorrow. Beyond this constant stream from outside, the House of Lords has to contend with the fundamental principle of heredity, which does not of necessity imply special ability.'

He wrote of Lord Salisbury's 'contempt for his fellow-men. Honestly and unaffectedly, he does not know why at least one-half of them exist'. He explained why Parliamentary proceedings had become generally more protracted. It was because extensions of the telegraph system enabled speeches to be printed in full in local newspapers, where formerly they were restricted to 'curt paragraphs'. Members had not found it worth while contributing substantially to debates that would not be reported in the constituencies. 'The altered circumstances,' Lucy observed, 'are responsible for much loquacity at Westminster.'

A *Strand Magazine* writer of greater renown had entered the political arena as Conservative candidate for Edinburgh Central. 'If anyone asks me my real reason for doing so,' Conan Doyle admitted, 'I should find it difficult to give them an intelligent answer. It was certainly not from any burning desire to join that august assembly.' He was defeated, as a result, he believed, of the propaganda of an Evangelical fanatic who put it about that he was educated by the Jesuits.

Lucy noted 'a rush of novelists into this new field of action', naming Conan Doyle, Anthony Hope, and Gilbert Parker. He added the information, slightly more surprising now than it may have been then, that 'Mr Barrie coquetted with a constituency, but came to the conclusion that he would bide a wee'. According to *The Sketch*, 'Mr Kipling has thought of going into the House of Commons'. The number of journalists and newspaper proprietors involved in the first general election of the twentieth century was unusually high. Thirty-three were returned to Parliament, including Sir George Newnes for Swansea Town.

The composition of Parliament was changing, like so much else in that exciting decade. Lucy had heard Gladstone say that he knew a time when there were 'no more than four or five men of business' among the 600 members.

2

Regular features like *Portraits of Celebrities* and *From Behind The Speaker's Chair* had much to do with consolidating the circulation and prestige of the magazine in those years. They were the built-in attractions, as we would say now, buttresses of the loyalty of older readers who were nervous of change. There was another series that may have been even more effective as a pillar of the established *Strand* order. It was called *Illustrated Interviews*.

Stead, at the *Pall Mall Gazette*, had raised the newspaper interview to its highest peak of prominence in the history of journalism. *Illustrated Interviews* in *The Strand* introduced a new dimension, aided by the camera. Readers were put on a footing of intimacy with the famous men and women interviewed in articles that respected the civilities without being subservient to them.

Cardinal Manning's study was described with the exclamatory emphasis of a discovery. 'What a litter! Papers and pamphlets are scattered all over the place. Letters, bearing the postmark of every quarter of the globe, lie in a heap, waiting to be opened.' The aged, once ambitious and politically sagacious prelate was made to seem all too poignantly human as he posed for what proved to be the last photograph ever taken of him.

Waiting while the cameraman fumbled under his hooded

apparatus, the Cardinal pointed to a painting of High Mass in St Peter's and told the interviewer: 'The artist died before he had time to light the wicks of the altar candles.' Nearby on a table under glass was the white silk mitre of St Thomas à Becket, its gilt edging still faintly showing. For most people it was a new experience to read about eminent persons in such a clear light.

'Mr Irving is one of the few actors who, at the conclusion of a death scene in a tragedy, always falls forward. He has taken the opinion of physicians and old soldiers on the subject, and it is the only natural way with those suddenly overtaken by death.'

In rooms on No. 7 staircase at Christ Church, Oxford, the interviewer finds Lewis Carroll (Charles Lutwidge Dodgson). 'With all his humour, he takes a very serious view of life and has a grave vein running through his mind. The simplicity of his faith, his deep reverence, and his childlike trust in the goodness of God are very striking.' Asked about recreation, the author of *Alice in Wonderland* answers that he sought it in the theatre. 'With his strict views of morality, and refined taste, Mr Dodgson has often been able to induce stage managers to correct, or omit, anything that might jar on sensitive ears.'

Interviewed at Graems Dyke, Harrow Weald, W. S. Gilbert, revealed that when he and Sullivan first went into partnership 'the burlesque stage was in a very unclean state. We made up our minds to do all we could to wipe out the grosser elements, never to let an offending word escape our characters, and never to allow a man to appear as a woman or *vice versa*'. *The Yeomen of the Guard*, he said, was suggested by 'an advertisement of The Times Furnishing Company at Uxbridge Station'. When the interviewer remarked on the two parrots in the house, Gilbert replied: 'Yes, the older bird takes in pupils.' He mentioned that he was born at 17 Southampton Street, Strand, and that his grandfather had known Johnson, Garrick, and Reynolds.

Jules Verne warmed the hearts of Mudies' subscribers by informing *The Strand* interviewer that in his opinion Englishmen make the best heroes in fiction. Interviewed in his consulting-room in Cavendish Square, W., Sir Morell Mackenzie, the celebrated surgeon who operated on the Emperor Frederick of Germany for cancer of the throat, cautioned readers against the risks of excessive cigarette smoking.

Sir George Lewis, 'the eminent solicitor', who was born in the room that was subsequently his private office at Ely Place, Holborn, was visited at his weekend house, Ashley Cottage, Walton-on-Thames. He spoke of Charles Stewart Parnell, 'a man of the most secretive, suspicious and distrustful disposition. He trusted few', though Lewis acknowledged him as a 'man of immense power, possessing the mind of a statesman, and indeed a very great Irishman'.

Sir George told of his efforts over many months to secure Parnell's confidence. They had a long and earnest conversation on Walton-on-Thames railway station. 'Noticing his anxiety, I put out my hand and said to him: "You can trust me as you could your brother." We shook hands earnestly but somehow I do not think I gained what I wanted.'

Sir George Lewis's professional standing was of the highest. At his house in Portland Place, his study was 'packed with gifts from grateful clients'. The interviewer wrote: 'Without a trace of egotism in his tone, he said: "Let me tell you that no novel was ever written, no play ever produced, that has or could contain such incidents and situations as at the present moment are securely locked up in the archives of memory which no one will ever discover."' It was a kind of ponderous pronouncement that was impressive sixty years ago when most people were still in thrall to the social concept of 'our betters'.

Their awe was probably deepened by the disclosure that Sir George had told *The Strand Magazine* 'in confidence' the name of the poisoner in the famous Bravo case. His lasting memory of the 'baccarat scandal' of 1891 was, he said, Lord Justice Coleridge's charge to the jury: 'Gentlemen, in considering the honour of Sir William Gordon Cumming,'—the plaintiff—'do not forget your own.'

It was Sir George Lewis who, in a rare epigrammatic flash said that 'the indiscretions of biographers have added a new terror to death'. Sensation-seeking writers can have found no profit in a study of *Illustrated Interviews*. Their didactic tone, and the absence of the Plutarchian touch in the choice of subjects, may explain why less fanatical researchers have made little use of them as source or reference material. For readers they had an almost spellbinding attraction, bringing the high and mighty into unfamiliar focus and confirming the hope that, after all, they were as human as the more common order of men.

Before me, as I sat at the editorial desk, was the bookcase in which Greenhough Smith's Cambridge-blue bound volumes of the magazine were kept through his forty years as editor. They were a rich repository of information about their successive decades, of many aspects of which they preserved the authentic tone, much of it in *Illustrated Interviews*. It would be futile to look there or anywhere else in *The Strand Magazine* of those first years of the century for any sign of the masochistic self-depreciation that has since overcome us.

One of the illustrations for *My Escape from the Boers*, by Winston
Churchill, published in *The Strand Magazine*, December 1923.

Early contributors to *The Strand Magazine:* (Top) W. Somerset
Maugham in 1909; (left) Arthur Morrison; and Henry Dudeney,
who conducted *Perplexities*, a famous *Strand* regular feature.

TEN

Famous 'Strand' Story Writers

I

Many hearts quickened with pleasure at the announcement printed in *The Strand* of September 1903: 'Readers have a vivid recollection of the time when Sherlock Holmes made his first appearance before the public, and of the *Adventures* which made his name a household word in every quarter of the world. The news of his death was received with regret as at the loss of a personal friend. Fortunately, the news, though based on circumstantial evidence which at the time seemed conclusive, turns out to be erroneous. How he escaped from his struggle with Moriarty at the Reichenbach Falls, why he remained in hiding even from his friend Watson, how he made his reappearance, and the manner he signalised his return by one of the most remarkable of his exploits will be found in the first story of the New Series, beginning in the October Number.'

In the dark interval various ways of keeping his memory green had been devised. 'Let's Keep Holmes Alive' clubs were formed in San Francisco, Chicago, and Boston. They sprang up in other cities and towns. The American novelist, Christopher Morley, then on the staff of the *Saturday Review of Literature*, was a prime mover in the formation of The Baker Street Irregulars, a name derived from the amateurs on whom from time to time Holmes called for help in his investigations. The Irregulars sired their own outlying groups dedicated to the perpetuation of Holmes as a figure of awesome regard. They issued a quarterly magazine, the *Baker Street Journal*.

During that same period of the 1930s, the Sherlock Holmes Society of London was founded. Among its original members were a future president of the Royal Academy, Sir Gerald Kelly, R.A., and the Master of a Cambridge college, Sir Sydney Roberts. Revived after the Second World War, the Society had 250 members in 1961.

The return of Sherlock Holmes in 1903 produced a flood of letters for him 'care of Sir Arthur Conan Doyle'. Those that were not addressed 'Sir Sherlock Holmes' used the polite form of 'Sherlock Holmes, Esq.' Most were requests for his autograph, some for signed photographs. There were appeals for copies of his family tree and coat-of-arms. More embarrassing personally to Conan Doyle were the gifts of tobacco, pipe cleaners, violin strings, intended to be passed on to his detective. Conan Doyle himself was continually being asked to help in tracing missing relatives, wills, and the perpetrators of minor crimes.

Vexing Holmes problems were debated in the newspapers. Was Dr Watson twice married? Just what had Holmes been doing, after the disposal of Moriarty at the Falls, in that baffling interregnum known to the elect as The Hiatus?

The Turks in 1920 believed him capable of being up to no good in their affairs. A correspondent of *The Times* reported from Constantinople that they had suspicions that 'the great English detective, Sherlock Holmes', was active behind the scenes in the politics of Asia Minor.

Conan Doyle wrote in his *Memories and Adventures*: 'They say a man is never appreciated until he is dead, and the general protest against my summary execution of Holmes taught me how many and how numerous were his friends. I heard of many who wept. I fear I was utterly callous myself.' He also wrote in the same place: 'I do not think that I ever realised what a living actual personality Holmes had become to the more guileless readers, until I heard of the very pleasing story of the char-a-banc of French schoolboys who, when asked what they wanted to see first in London, replied unanimously that they wanted to see Mr Holmes's lodgings in Baker Street.'

He may have been still more gratified by the amount of attention given to the Holmes stories as intellectual exercises. As early as 1912, Ronald Knox wrote a treatise, *Studies in the*

Literature of Sherlock Holmes. It was followed by S. C. Roberts's *Dr Watson* (1931), T. S. Blakeney's *Sherlock Holmes: Fact or Fiction* (1932), and Vincent Starrett's *Private Life of Sherlock Holmes* (1961).

Whether or not they are seen as moves in an elaborate game, those substantial additions to the Holmes canon testify to a vitality that has passed from the surprising to the inexplicable. The process was accelerated by the recent re-naming of a 'pub' in Northumberland Street, London, W.C., as the 'Sherlock Holmes', and its solemn dedication as a head-quarters of a cult that in its origins had no affinity with the saloon bar.

The first story in the new series was *The Adventure of the Empty House*. 'It was in the spring of the year 1894 that all London was interested, and the fashionable world dismayed, by the murder of the Honourable Robert Adair.' As Holmes would say, 'The game's afoot again, Watson', and readers rushed to the bookstalls with the fierce resolve of shoppers at the January sales. It was as if they unconsciously resented the new era, dreading its hidden possibilities, and longed to return to the safer and saner past. For them it was only yesterday and already it had an easeful period charm that could be savoured again in the pages of *The Strand Magazine* of 1903–4.

They were credulous and uncritical. None apparently noticed that in *The Final Problem*, for example, Dr Watson had not heard of Moriarty, while in *The Valley of Fear*, published earlier, it was clear that he knew of the professor's existence.

In *A Study in Scarlet* Watson remarks on Holmes's cultural limitations. 'Of contemporary history, philosophy and politics he appeared to know next to nothing. Upon my quoting Thomas Carlyle, he inquired in the naivest way who he might be and what he had done.' In *The Sign of Four*, Holmes recommends to Watson the study of Winwood Reade's *Martyrdom of Man*, cites French epigrams, and quotes Goethe. Elsewhere, he exhibits a knowledge of Horace and George Sand.

Conan Doyle's scientific training was answerable for a large part of his success with Sherlock Holmes. He showed ineptitude in certain matters of scientific detail, supplying, unwittingly, the humour in more than one of what Holmes called 'medicated stories', those collected under the title of *Round the Red Lamp*. He had put up his plate as an oculist, yet gave one of his fiction characters, a near-sighted woman, convex glasses instead of the concave ones befitting her case.

When Greenhough Smith pointed out to him that in *The Lost World* the animal hide balloon could not have lifted its own weight, Conan Doyle riposted in a facetious mood. 'The gas was Levogen, a volcanic product peculiar to plateau conditions, which has been calculated by Prof. T. E. S. Tube, F.R.S., to be 35,371 times lighter than hydrogen.'

An unexpected sequel to the Holmes revival was the extraordinary success of the new series with the French reading public, on which previously Conan Doyle and his detective had made no great impression. A Paris newspaper, reporting a case of murder, printed an imaginary interview with Sherlock Holmes, not at all to the delight of the Paris police. It was the signal for something like a Holmes *furore* over there. The stories were printed and reprinted in serial and book form. A French adaptation of the Holmes play made famous in America by William Gillette played to packed houses at the Théâtre Antoine. A newspaper correspondent wrote that 'every other boulevard *flâneur* considers himself a Sherlock Holmes and goes about applying the science of deduction to the little problems of his daily life'.

In London, during the Holmes heyday, devotees were seen queuing at one of the largest public libraries for the chance of reading the latest story in the series. So pressing was the demand that closing time at the library was extended by half an hour on *The Strand* publication day, usually the third Thursday in the month.

2

Three contributors to *The Strand* were named in the book gossip columns as the most highly paid writers of the day, Conan Doyle, Stanley Weyman, and S. R. Crockett. Doyle's 'man of business', as he called him, was A. P. Watt, one of the first literary agents to build up a practice akin to that of a prosperous solicitor. He started as a young manuscript reader in a publishing office managed by his brother-in-law, named Strahan. The business declined and Watt saw that he would soon be looking for a job. Meanwhile, he helped a friend to get a book accepted by another publisher. It then struck him that there was probably work of that sort to be done on a commission basis. The field was wide open. Soon he was acting for some of the most successful authors; for instance, Kipling and Anthony Hope, as well as Conan Doyle.

He could tell prospective clients of an author foolishly selling all his rights in a new book for £500 and of the publisher making a profit of £19,000 from the transaction. He could have pointed out that he would not have let Thomas Hardy make contracts that gave his publishers one-third of his serial rights. His position as an agent was strengthened by the insistence of Sir Walter Besant, chairman of the Society of Authors, that as a class authors were poor business men and at the mercy of the more buccaneering publishers. The conclusion of the copyright agreement with the United States was also in Watt's favour. It put an end to injustices that Dickens so bitterly resented and made the services of a reliable go-between invaluable to British writers whose work was of interest to American publishers.

Dr Robertson Nicoll reviewed the new profession in *The Bookman*. 'Next to no capital is required,' he wrote, 'there are no losses, the expenses of conducting an office are very small. When a transaction is completed, it continues to yield a result for years and years. The most profitable transactions are the easiest. To sell the books of a popular novelist is not hard, and the lucky man of business enjoys a royalty upon every copy sold during the whole period of copyright. . . . I know one novelist whose income next year will be very little if at all under £10,000. In return for transacting his business, the literary agent receives the handsome sum of nearly £1,000, and his clients, it must be remembered, are very numerous. No losses have to be set against these gains.'

The assessment was not wholly realistic. It took no account

of the financial aid given by some literary agents, Watt probably among them, to authors awaiting recognition and royalties. Before Arnold Bennett, a prominent contributor to *The
Strand* in the 1920s, made his name with *The Old Wives' Tale*,
he was largely supported by funds provided by his agent,
J. B. Pinker, to whom he remained loyal through the rest of
his career.

Of A. P. Watt, Conan Doyle wrote as he looked back to the
time when as a young doctor he put up his plate at 2 Devonshire Place, W., and filled in the blank hours by writing
stories: 'He relieved me of all hateful bargaining, and handled
things so well that any immediate anxiety for money soon
disappeared. It was as well, for not one single patient had
ever crossed the threshold of my room.'[1]

3

Stanley Weyman (1855–1928), a *Strand* author from the first
number, succeeded in the sphere of the historical novel to a
degree that Conan Doyle would have envied, had he not been
singularly free from the base emotions. *A Gentleman of
France*, *Under The Red Robe*, *The Red Cockade*, were considered to be 'as good as anything by Dumas', which meant
that they provided unequivocal answers to certain questions.
Does the reader live in the story? Does he share love, hate,
fear, hope, despair, with the characters in it? Does he shud-
der when death comes close? Does he feel relief when danger
passes? In the stories of Weyman (pronounced Wyman) the
answer was rarely in doubt: yes.

There were exaggerated coincidences, made-to-measure
heroines, time-honoured situations. There was also an infusion
of scholarship entitling Weyman's richly brocaded romances
to more critical respect than they received. The standard of
reviewing usually applied to his work was epitomised in the
hackneyed comment: 'Another of this author's well-spun
yarns.'

Weyman had an exacting historical sense, though he astonished a friend who stood with him on the topmost stones of

[1] Sir Arthur Conan Doyle: *Memories and Adventures.*

the ruins of Ludlow Castle when he remarked: 'I see no romance in English history. That is why I go to France for my stories.' His social conscience was somewhat rigid, perhaps not unexpectedly so in an author who wore a frock-coat, a monocle, and cultivated a minor replica of Lord Kitchener's moustache. It allowed him to indulge the fancy that dash and daring were exclusive to the high-born and that rascality was more or less confined to the lower orders of mankind.

He was the son of a Shropshire solicitor. After Shrewsbury School and Cambridge, he read for the Bar. He was discouraged by losing his first case, in which he acted for Charles Dickens, junior, the plaintiff. His earnings averaged £130 a year. Feeling 'a complete failure', he went back to live with his mother and sister in the house at Ludlow that he was born in. There he started to write, for some years with little success.

A short story of his was accepted for *The Cornhill Magazine*. James Payn, the editor, urged him to try his hand at a longer work, a novel on an historical theme. He went away emboldened to do so and produced *A Gentleman of France*.

Weyman's books subsequently sold in great numbers at home and abroad. Among his admirers was Oscar Wilde, who believed that the stories were good for the morale of his fellow prisoners in Reading Gaol. By 1908, after no more than ten years' labour, he had made enough money to retire to a quiet life at Ruthin, Denbighshire, where he was chairman of the bench of magistrates.

In ten more years his name reappeared in a publisher's list, his earlier works having gone on selling meanwhile in numerous editions. His hand had not lost its skill. By the time of his death, at the end of a further ten years' span, he had provided an abundance of delight for a world-wide republic of readers and had earned his title to remembrance with the masters of the art of historical romance writing.

The Raiders, that resounding tale of eighteenth-century Scottish outlaws and gypsies, and the succession of other romances from the pen of Samuel Rutherford Crockett (1860–1914) gave him, too, a place of honour in a great tradition Known as 'The Covenanter novelist', he bowed the head to

Scott and Stevenson. He had a natural gift for narrative and he exercised it with infectious vigour. One could imagine him sitting on a Scottish hillside shouting his inventions to the wind. Physically, he was an imposing sight, six feet four, powerfully built, with the beard of a patriarch even in his twenties. Behind the robust front was a quick mind and a cheerful temper. Life for Crockett was 'good and glad and full of joyful surprise'. He had a poetically sensitive eye for the beauty of the earth and especially for his Galloway homeland and the Solway shore.

For ten years he was a Free Church minister, ordained after reading science at Edinburgh University, whither he had worked his way from a local school as a tenant farmer's son. He resigned his pastorate to write novels. For most of his life, through all seasons, he never missed a sunrise. Emulating Sir Walter, he began writing at 5 a.m. He would do four hours' work at his desk and spend the rest of the day outdoors with field glasses, a devoted watcher of the natural scene in his native countryside. Two researchers were constantly employed on his behalf in the libraries and muniment rooms of Scotland. In one year, 1897, he had on hand commissions for seven new novels and fifty magazine stories.

Gladstone corresponded with him, so did Rosebery: both admirers of his. Kitchener read one of his books, *The Grey Man*, before going to sleep on the night before the battle of Omdurman. Crockett belongs so completely to his period that one is surprised to find that he was a regular user of the then new Edison Bell phonograph for dictation purposes 'to lighten the labours of the day'. I have seen a letter, dated April 3, 1895, in which he wrote appreciatively of that instrument. 'It enables me to sit down to work without having the edge taken off one's capacity by a couple of hours' correspondence. I should not like to be without it.'

4

New authors' names were appearing in *The Strand* index: Robert Barr, William (not yet contracted to W.) Somerset Maugham, P. G. Wodehouse, Barry Pain, Anthony Hope, Max

Pemberton ('the English Jules Verne'), Jerome K. Jerome ('the English Mark Twain'), A. E. W. Mason, H. Seton Merriman, E. W. Hornung. Three of them outlived the magazine, Mason, Maugham, and Wodehouse, and wrote for it over a wide span of years.

Although in the jargon of the circulation men he never 'sold copies', Maugham was the most competent if not the most accomplished. No popular story writer for *The Strand* had a more thorough mastery of the business. His first story in the magazine was *A Point of Law*. It brought him £20, enough for a much-needed holiday on the Riviera at a time when he was not doing very well. After that, *The Strand* always had a warm place in his regard.

Wodehouse gained so strong a hold on the readers that his name was often given the premier front-cover position, the 'banner line' at the top. That was in the '30s. Long before, he had contributed cricket stories to the magazine, his first involving the mental pose of an adolescent girl: 'It is a splendid thing to be seventeen and have one's hair up and feel that one cannot be kissed indiscriminately any more by sticky boys and horrid old gentlemen. . . .'

One reads that first-person story, called *The Wirepullers*, with a slight apprehension of its having some hidden morbid significance. One tries to make it fit Wodehouse's subsequent frank avowal that 'mentally, I seem not to have progressed a step since I was 18'.[1] One guesses at the relevance of Arnold Bennett's diary note, after dining with Wodehouse and an American publisher at the Savoy many years later: ' "P.G." is a very queer modest man.'

Kirkegaard believed that the comic sense has its strongest roots in suffering. The relative smoothness of Wodehouse's course through a long working life meant that he has been merely funny, all that his readers ask. In his confessional vein, he said: 'I feel I've been fooling the public for fifty years.'[2] That justifies Arnold Bennett's second adjective but tells us little more about Wodehouse, who has also said: 'I don't know anything and I seem incapable of learning.' His first

[1] *Performing Flea: A Self-Portrait in Letters* (Jenkins, 1953).
[2] *Ibid.*

short stories were published in the Newnes schoolboys' monthly, *The Captain*, long defunct. There are those who would say that he has been writing for a ghostly version of it ever since.

Some of his earlier *Strand* stories were written in partnership with C. H. Bovill, a short story and lyric writer who, having more work in hand than he could do, wrote to Wodehouse, then contributing to a London evening newspaper column, suggesting collaboration. Bovill's son has written: 'My father liked his style. He came to live in our flat at 94 Prince of Wales Mansions, S.W., for two years, where they got to work.'[1] In the First World War, C. H. Bovill joined the Coldstream Guards and died of wounds in 1918. Wodehouse went to America.

'By Robert Barr' at the top of a page always stirred expectations of more than passing entertainment. The name appeared over a number of well-wrought stories in *The Strand*. Glasgow-born, sometime headmaster of the Public School, Windsor, Ontario, Barr was the London representative of the *Detroit Free Press*. He shared Kipling's chambers in Villiers Street, Strand. He became co-editor of *The Idler* with Jerome K. Jerome. When they decided to dissolve the partnership, Barr wrote novels that, not for want of merit, have long been dusty on the shelves.

That fate awaited too many *Strand* writers: H. Seton Merriman, author of *The Sowers*, Frankfort Moore, whose friends laughed behind their hands when he told them that he finished his novel, *The Jessamy Bride*, 'in a mist of tears', Sir Gilbert Parker, who wrote tales of the Great North-West, H. B. Marriott-Watson, from Australia, who also had his little hour as novelist and short story writer: one of Henley's 'young men', remembered also for his striking head of hair, 'like an Assyrian king's'.

H. Seton Merriman deserved more than that passing glance as one of the most able and popular fiction writers of the turn of the century. He was the author of eighteen novels, among them *The Sowers*, *Barlasch of the Guard*, and *In Kedar's Tents*, that gained him a wide and steadfast public who were moved

[1] Mr Charles Bovill, in a letter, October 23, 1964.

by the disclosure that his death, aged 40 in 1903, was the culmination of a dread that shadowed his life. He was a nephew of W. L. Thomas, founder of *The Graphic*, the first of London's illustrated newspapers. Avoiding literary circles, Merriman held firmly to the view that an author should be known only by his work. Almost his last injunction as a dying man was that there should be no public mention of his illness or death. His closest friendship seems to have been with Stanley Weyman, himself one of the most reticent of novelists.

For a time, Merriman was a Lloyds underwriter. He was in a position to travel extensively, using his experiences and impressions (and also, to the distaste of some critics, his reflections) co-extensively in his stories. He was a disciple of Flaubert and the French clarity of thought pervades his writing, though precision of language does not. Strength of plot and careful character drawing override his lack of stylistic distinction. The dignified tone of his work was pleasing to many readers.

Morley Roberts, another *Strand* name from the '90s, has been called 'the last eminent Victorian'.[1] His voice was often raised in denunciation of the 'lack of guts' in modern literature. He was a practised craftsman who had something to say and always said it with force. At the Authors' Club, where he was a shining light, he asserted a didactic tyranny that made timorous members shy away from his presence. He wrote seventy books without becoming a hack.

5

Two writers for the magazine who have been more generously treated by posterity were Anthony Hope (1863–1933) and A. E. W. Mason (1865–1948). Hope, whose family name was Hawkins, had his rocket blast of fame when *The Strand* was three years old. He was at the Bar and living with his widower father, the rector of St Bride's, Fleet Street. 'He seemed to be marked out perfectly for a career of dull and learned respectability.'[2] As a young barrister, he devilled for

[1] Oliver Edwards: 'Up From Avernus'; *The Times*. April 29, 1965.
[2] *The Strand Magazine*, vol. 31: *Portraits of Celebrities At Different Ages*.

a future Prime Minister, H. H. Asquith, and held good briefs for the Great Western Railway Company. In idle hours in chambers he discovered a facility for story writing and exerted himself to produce one or two novels, the first published at his own expense and at a loss to him of £30. One was an intended satire on democracy. He had time also to stand for Parliament, which he was not destined to enter.

Walking home to 16 Buckingham Street, Strand, from Westminster county court, where he had that afternoon won a case, he passed two men so alike that they started his mind working on complications that might be devised for just such a pair in a more romantic setting than the Thames Embankment. The next day, November 29, 1893, he sat down to write *The Prisoner of Zenda*. It was finished as a first draft in four weeks.

Six months later he gave notice by letter to his legal clients and colleagues of his intention to quit the Bar, and settled down to twenty prosperous years as a novelist and playwright. By then he was working out the plot of another great success, *Rupert of Hentzau*.

His *Dolly Dialogues* (1894) give the impression that he was an Edwardian in the wrong decade. Long since grown brittle with age, they were exercises in the distinguished persiflage of the Stafford House soirées and other great social occasions of the brief reign to come. Anthony Hope was himself a much-liked figure in society; a drawling dandy with a priest-like face who carried himself with an air of inherited professionalism. 'He goes everywhere, is seen everywhere, speaks everywhere, and says kind things everywhere to everyone who reads him.'[1]

Every day he went to his desk from ten till one, sitting with pen in hand, whether or not ideas and ink combined in a productive flow. Like Dickens, like Wells, he was not intimidated by the blank page. There were days when he wrote nothing, others when his pen raced to keep up with his adroit rather than powerful imagination. It was characteristic of him that when *The Strand* turned down a set of short stories specially written for it round a central figure called Count Antonio, he

[1] *Ibid.*

showed no hurt feelings and at once offered to write another series with a different theme.

He was highly successful with his 'reading' tours in the United States, where admiration for him was widespread through all ranks of society. A New York hostess privately offered him £500 if he would choose her drawing-room as the scene of his first social appearance in that city. On a train to Boston, the dining-car attendant seized a chicken bone from Hope's lunch plate, announcing that he intended having it polished to present to his lady-love.

His own prominent place in London society, where he was on terms of close friendship with at least one duchess (Her Grace of Sutherland), did not preclude him from recognising the superior merits of its equivalent in New York life. There he found more hostesses of high degree whose doors were opened to artists, musicians, and writers, and there, too, he could report, money was not necessarily the pass-word as it mostly was in Edwardian London. For him, American society was 'just about right; gay, animated and luxurious, but not feverish nor of an overdone sumptuousness'.

Returning from one of his American tours, he met on ship-board, and subsequently married, at his father's church in Fleet Street, Betty Sheldon, the daughter of a New York business man. She was 18 to his 40. They set up house at 41 Bedford Square, London, W.C.1. When Hope died in 1933, Sir James Barrie dashed off the impulsively generous epitaph that 'he made more people happy than any other author of our time'.

Notes that I made between the wars refresh my memory of A. E. W. Mason, whom I described as 'one of the last of our great tribal story-tellers'. I see that I went on to assert that 'their gifts of robust narrative, their heroic imaginations, their individual air of being story-primate of all-England, and their scorn for the more subtle insinuations of modern publicity methods, made their successors look like lepidoptera beside mastodons' (written just after he had left my office in Fleet Street). As an editor, beset by the thin-necked neurotic school of writers, I felt like crying out, as the Northern captain did when General Grant was given his command before Vicksburg: 'At last! At last! At last a man!'

I noted Mason's 'quarter-deck style', that he was tall and sunburnt, that he dropped endings of words, and that he wore a monocle 'with rather less affectation than most who flaunt that ornament at us'. He gave an impression 'of having had a solidly comfortable, good life', and he remains in my memory as a fine-featured fellow who looked like a retired, still briskly active, admiral. As for the good life, 'Mason has an air of having enjoyed it to the last drop—yachts, House of Commons, plentiful travel, a country home, the Garrick Club, and any number of devoted friends'.

He wrote half a dozen novels before *The Four Feathers*, set in the Sudan and serialised in *The Cornhill*, bore him up to the best-seller heights in 1902. That, and *No Other Tiger*, *Fire Over England*, *Musk and Amber*, and *The House in Lordship Lane*, are the best remembered of his thirty or more book titles. He wrote many short stories and had half a dozen plays staged in the West End, including *At The Villa Rose* at the Strand Theatre; *Running Water* at Wyndham's; *No Other Tiger* at the St James'. He had once been ambitious to shine as an actor.

More successful in his political activities than his friend Anthony Hope, he entered the House of Commons as member for Coventry in the great Liberal avalanche of 1906. Barrie and E. V. Lucas went to some of his election meetings, at which Mason was seen frequently turning aside to use a throat-spray. 'He is loved all over the place,' Barrie wrote to tell Quiller-Couch ('Q' of the Cornish novels). 'He is as big a swell as ever, but his socks don't match and so all is well.' Barrie's phrase, 'a big swell', fitted Mason. Anthony Hope considered him 'a notable fellow', in which it is also easy to concur from brief acquaintance. One of his friends was Captain Scott, the Polar explorer, who may have supplied some of the character-isation, if not the inspiration, for his novel called *The Turnstile*.

Mason had the thing called presence, that mysterious emana-tion, always rare, now almost gone, one sometimes feels, from the human ethos. In memory I bracket him with C. B. Fry, they had so much of the same form and style and personal amplitude, and also the same memorable tone of voice.

Mason's laugh rings down the years. He seems now to have been one of the last to laugh with head thrown back as if in high exultation. He wrote for *The Strand* very nearly from its beginning and his last published story appeared very near its end. There are aspects of his work that seem to foreshadow James Bond, though Mason certainly never saw himself in the role of professional sadist.

He lived to be eighty-four and among other distinctions he could claim to have declined one, a knighthood for 'services to literature'. He was said to have suffered a crushing disappointment when Edna May, the star of *The Belle of New York*, refused to marry him. Years later, when Mason was in his early sixties, Arnold Bennett saw him broken by grief at the impending inevitable fate of a young woman of whom he was extremely fond. Mostly, life was kind to him and through him to his friends.

6

Sustained by the vitality of *The Scarlet Pimpernel*, the name of Baroness Orczy remains fresh in the memory of old readers of *The Strand*. She was a Hungarian, her father a diplomat who became director of the National Opera House at Budapest. She was trained as an artist, aspiring to be another Angelica Kauffman. In London, she exhibited at the Royal Academy. She did illustrations for Raphael Tuck's children's books and for some of the minor Newnes publications.

She married a black-and-white artist named Montagu Barstow, who worked for the lighthearted penny weekly called *Pick-Me-Up*. She had never taken a pen in hand except to write letters. Her first try at story writing was successful with *Pearson's Magazine*, closest rival of *The Strand*.

The Scarlet Pimpernel was originally a play, 'written, accepted, and produced (tentatively in the provinces) all within nine months. I was then only a writer of magazine stories and knew not a soul connected with the stage'. With Julia Neilson and Fred Terry playing the chief parts, *The Scarlet*

Pimpernel became a great success, trebling the price per thousand words of everything that its author wrote thereafter.

Baroness Orczy once gave it out that Bret Harte had been a formative influence in her writing life. The photographs of her in her best years, her bold-bosomed presence crowned by the magnificent hats of the brief Edwardian interlude, made it hard to accept the likelihood that she had been even casually acquainted with *The Luck of Roaring Camp and Other Sketches.* If she was never one of the great story-tellers, she was of the company of those who held to the warm-hearted, generous tradition of the masters in the *genre.*

That was the era of the famous serial writing partnerships, literary double-acts topping the bill in the commercial fiction arena : C. N. and A. M. Williamson; Alice and Claude Askew; Agnes and Egerton Castle; Heath Hosken and Coralie Stanton. The Williamsons—he, sometime editor of the pioneer weekly picture paper, *Black-and-White*; she, the former Alice Livingston of New York—established themselves in the public favour with *The Lightning Conductor,* one of the first novels of the motoring age. Totally unreadable now, even as a period piece, it is cherished in my memory for the mental relief it provided in the front line at Festubert, 1915. They were adept pluralists of the market place, who in one year, 1908, wrote seven serial stories simultaneously for newspapers and magazines.

The Castles, husband and wife, produced a superior quality of fiction by the yard, much of it based on Egerton Castle's early travels and romantic tastes, indulged in the company of his well-to-do father, the founder of the *Liverpool Mercury.* Egerton Castle, M.A. (1858–1920) was a Sandhurst-trained professional soldier. He became one of Europe's best swordsmen; in his day, the only foreigner to be elected to the French Académie d'Armes. He was captain of the British épée and sabre teams at the Olympic Games of 1908.

When he married Agnes Sweetman, of Lamberton Park, Queen's County, Ireland, he joined the editorial staff of the *Saturday Review.* Later, he was a director of the Liverpool newspaper group that took over his father's paper. His fiction writing career was launched with a spare-time translation of a French novel. From then on, the Castle literary partnership

H. Greenhough Smith, editor of *The Strand Magazine* for forty years.

H. G. Wells in 1902. Some of the best of his early work appeared in *The Strand*.

Anthony Hope, *from a painting by Hugh T. de Glazebrook.*

Arnold Bennett at 'Godspeace', Witley, Surrey, in 1907; from a hitherto unpublished photograph.

developed into one of the most spectacular of its kind in the first decade of the century. Their names had the prominence of the film stars of the next generation. It was said that galley proofs of serial stories festooned every room of their London house, 49 Sloane Gardens, S.W.

Those gaily proficient providers of serials and short stories for *The Strand* and other magazines were pedestrian writers in a non-derogatory sense. Their feet were planted squarely on a common ground, where the surface was solid and familiar, where there was no need to look beyond the actual and the obvious. Occasionally, they may have raised their eyes to gaze on the summit of Parnassus. Mostly, they remained content with the surer profits to be earned by toiling on the lower slopes.

" ANTHEA PERSUADED THE OTHERS TO ALLOW HER TO HANG THE CHARM ROUND HER NECK."

One of H. R. Millar's illustrations for *The Amulet*, by E. Nesbit, serialised in *The Strand Magazine*.

ELEVEN

Wells and The Land Ironclads

I

Rhetoric, it seemed, could not be avoided in recording the early stages of the revolution on the roads that was to become a major fact of twentieth-century existence. 'The motor-car has entered our very stables and the corn-bin has been abolished by the petrol tank.' *The Strand* estimated that in 1903 there were twenty thousand motor vehicles in service, 'which involves the employment of twenty thousand drivers or chauffeurs'. Horses by the score were being sent from great country houses for auction at Tattersall's. 'A well-known baronet' had bought three motor cars and given notice to his coachman, groom, and stable boys. Men who had been with horses all their lives suddenly found themselves on the scrap heap, displaced by a new race of beings who wore leather jackets, goggles, and elbow-high gauntlet gloves.

The Strand reported that 'an indignation meeting' had been held at the Footmen's Club, at Brompton, S.W., where a candidate who had been seen on the front seat of a motor brougham was blackballed. Two years earlier the motorcar had not been thought worthy of mention in those pages. Now, 'Baron Henri de Rothschild has no doubt that in ten years there will not be a horse-drawn vehicle left in Paris'. And the magazine cautiously conjectured: 'May not the same also be prophetic of London?'

The Daimler Company, we learn from *The Strand* article, had established the first school of instruction for chauffeurs, just off Grays Inn Road. Some of the pupils arrived on horseback, tethering their mounts outside 'the excellently appointed garage'. A description is given of a typical morning's session. 'Now, what do you call this?' asks the instructor, pointing to the water-cooled brake drum. 'There is no reply from the assembled coachmen, grooms, and footmen. They scrutinise the intricate machine with despair pictured on their faces.'

That same year, H. G. Wells made in *The Strand* his fiction forecast of tanks as a secret weapon of the next great war. He called them 'land ironclads'. Another remarkable signal from the future was picked up by the magazine in an article on the possibilities of what was called 'aesthetic surgery', the reshaping of human cartilage and tissue to obviate facial and other disfigurements. It was one of the first indications given to English readers of developments that were later brought to perfection by Sir Harold Gillies, the eminent plastic surgeon, and integrated by him and his school into modern surgical science.

A Scheme for a Great National Monument, which filled six pages of the issue for April 1903, was put before readers with period grandiloquence. 'The Empire of Great and Greater Britain has attained a power and splendour probably hitherto unequalled in the history of the world. It is interesting to inquire what lasting records would be left behind by so great a kingdom at its present stage of development. What evidence would be forthcoming, say, in eight thousand years' time, for some future Flinders Petrie digging among the buried cities of the British Isles?'

The Albert Memorial was 'fast crumbling to ruin'. It seemed 'not unlikely that the greatest memorial we shall leave to distant ages will be our railroads, which form a great distinguishing feature of the nineteenth century. The marvellous cuttings and embankments will exist as long as the face of the country in which they are placed'. A more imposing monument, one which would enshrine the nation's culture, was proposed. 'What was possible in ancient Egypt should surely not be altogether impossible in modern Britain.' It might be made of brick, 'each brick valued at, say, a penny. It would then be possible for the humblest of our countrymen or countrywomen to contribute a brick to the great monument'.

'L'Art Nouveau', which was the talk of Paris, and afterwards of London, in the middle Edwardian years: was it 'the voluptuous flowering of the highest artistic sense' claimed for it by its protagonists? 'We are to have not only New Art teapots, but New Art motorcars, New Art coal-scuttles, and New Art perambulators,' from which *The Strand* article predicted 'a steamroller which shall be a delight to look upon', the Scotch express being drawn up to Edinburgh by a beautiful bronze and enamel swan-shaped engine, factory chimneys rising into the sky like the decorated capitals of a temple dedicated to the highest refinements of the human spirit.

Invited to state their opinions, Hamo Thornycroft, R.A., deemed 'l'Art Nouveau' to be 'an honest expression of the age', Goscombe John, A.R.A., anticipated that 'what is valuable in it will be absorbed, giving vitality to what in many directions has become conventional and dead', while Alfred Gilbert, R.A., dismissed it as 'absolute nonsense—it belongs to the young ladies' seminary and the duffers' paradise'. Seymour Lucas, R.A., and Arnesby Brown, A.R.A., believed in the future of the movement. 'It is noticeable', concluded *The Strand* survey, 'that the architects seem dead against it.'

The symposium journalism of *The Strand* anticipated the 'Brains Trust' programmes of radio and television. It broadcast the opinions of notable experts on topics of more than casual interest. The views of the distinguished medical men who answered questions on the nation's health in 1906 can still be read with profit. They all condemned over-eating, under-exercising, over-weight. 'Eating to satisfy hunger is a different matter from eating to gratify the palate.' They regarded fat as a disease, and considered that twelve ounces of food a day was sufficient for the average person, subject to its quality. Walking was the ideal exercise. 'A matter of the first importance is the air we breathe—it should be free from gaseous or solid filth.'

Dr J. Milson Rhodes, of Didsbury, Manchester, chairman of the Central Committee of Poor Law Conferences for England and Wales, did not agree that there was physical degeneration among the English working classes. He cited statistical information which showed improvement over the previous three decades. 'The curse of the working classes is the way they are housed. Give the people houses to live in, not places to die in, and you will have done much to promote the healthy physical development of the nation.'

The doctors were critical of the tea-drinking habit. Dr W. K. Sibley, of Duke Street, Grosvenor Square, W., author of a book on the treatment of disease by light and heat, asserted that it was 'becoming almost as much a curse and cause of disease as alcohol'. Dr Andrew Wilson considered 'tea-bibbing a modern evil, though less harmful than alcohol or coffee'. Dr Yorke-Davies, of Harley Street, recommended that tea should be infused not longer than five minutes, and announced himself 'a strong advocate of teas grown in Ceylon'.

According to Dr C. W. Saleeby, 'author of *The Cycle of Life*, *Evolution the Master Key*, etc.', the astringent part of the tea leaf, known as tannin, has 'a wholly deleterious action upon the stomach and the functions of that organ. The ideal cup of tea contains a fair quantity of theine and no tannin whatever'. He advocated removing all the leaves from the pot after 'no more than four minutes' infusion, at the very outside'. Dr John Haddon, of Denholme, Roxburghshire, had never found in his practice any evidence that tea drinking does harm. 'I know one woman who for the last thirty years of her life lived on white bread toasted and tea, dying over eighty years of age.'

The subject of age was debated in another article in the light of the lengthening human span. 'Less than a century ago,' readers were reminded, 'a man was old at 40.' Jane Austen described men of 35 as middle-aged and those of 60 'as being in their dotage'. A noted physician of Edwardian society, Sir William Osler, was still 'writing off' the man of 60. 'Thereafter he is a negligible quantity.'

The Strand countered that professional view with the statement that 'if Lord Strathcona had died at 60 he would have been unknown to fame', as one of the builders of modern Canada. In his 90th year he was at his office every morning at ten o'clock and was rarely in bed before one a.m. Nor did Pierpont Morgan launch his greatest financial operation until he was 65. And Lord Roberts was nearly 70 when he was sent to South Africa to retrieve the mistakes of younger generals. Gladstone was impressively quoted. 'Had I died at three score years and ten, fully half my life's work would have remained undone.'

Readers were further reminded that Titian was working on his *Pietà* at 98, and that Corot painted two of his finest pictures in his 79th year. The case of Victor Hugo was cited, 'at 83 working on a new tragedy', and, what was not revealed to readers of *The Strand*, demonstrating his Promethean vitality in forays at the local brothel. A summing-up note was supplied by another prominent contemporary physician, Sir James Crichton Browne. 'Life owes every man and woman a hundred years. It is their business to see that they collect the debt.'

2

There was implied awareness of the precariousness of life but not of society. Catastrophe in various forms provided the climax of stories in which both dialogue and illustrations preserved the old class patterns. Parlourmaids still answered 'Yes, ma'am', with a quick curtsey to the mistress of the house, or 'No, Miss Amelia', to her daughter. Butlers still obviously had monarchical status below stairs. Footmen were still shown taking in cards on silver salvers.

Social justice was not a *Strand Magazine* theme. The views of Hyndman, Shaw, Russell, or of Wells, whose adventurous imagination continued to impart liveliness to its fiction, would have been hardly conducive to the relaxation that it was the editor's mission to provide. For instance, an article on the great metropolitan landlords may not have had more than an informative intent. That the facts it set forth were material for political dissidence could not be denied.

They showed that five square miles of London were owned by nine families, apart from the Crown and the City companies. The Duke of Westminster owned 400 acres, including Belgrave Square and much of Knightsbridge and Park Lane. The Cadogan estate consisted of 200 acres in and about Chelsea, the Portman estate of 270 acres in the region of Oxford Street and Baker Street. Lord Howard de Walden (aged 25) owned 290 acres in Marylebone and the Regent's Park district. Much of St John's Wood and Swiss Cottage belonged to the Eyre family, and a large part of Hampstead to the Maryon-Wilson family. The Pratt family (Marquess of Camden) were over-lords of Chalk Farm and Camden Town.

The oldest landlords of them all were the Bedford dukes, whose revenue from Covent Garden Market dues alone came to £25,000 a year, a minor item in the enormous income from their properties in and around Bloomsbury. South of the river, there was Lord Llangattock (the Rolls family), who took the rents from streets of houses and shops in Bermondsey, Southwark, and the Old Kent Road neighbourhood. Precisely drawn maps of the separate estates, each ringed to show their locale and extent, emphasised a land-owning monopoly that may have surprised some, and scandalised others, by its magnitude.

A *Strand* inquiry into divorce in the United Kingdom in 1910 (population 32,000,000) yielded statistical material that makes piquant reading against the background of our latter-day sophistication. The annual average over five years was 568. A table gave comparative figures for other countries: United States, 55,502; Japan, 93,949; France, 8,864; Germany, 8,680; Italy, 819; Ireland, 1.

3

As a lifelong Liberal, Sir George Newnes could hardly have objected to the publication of articles in his magazine that stimulated some degree of radical thought. In any event, he was by then an ailing man, a victim of diabetes and drink, whose misjudgments were alarming his colleagues of the company.

He had lost the fortune accruing to him from the 'healthy popular literature' that had brought him the esteem of the people and honour from the Sovereign. A venture in New South Wales, based on shale-oil operations, cost him £240,000. He had some success as a temporary partner of Northcliffe's young brother, Leicester Harmsworth, in promoting the Darracq motorcar in the British market. His gains largely disappeared with his heavy investment in Peruvian rubber. Between 1903 and 1910, he more than once stood on the edge of a financial precipice.

His impaired judgment led him into other speculative schemes in the City. He was induced to provide capital for a hammock-sprung motorcar seat, the 'Ever-clean collar' for men, and a device to equip motorcar wheels with springs in place of pneumatic tyres.

Some of his latest plans for new publications were hopelessly at variance with the popular demand. He was persuaded to engage in ill-starred plans of major proportions in the book-publishing field, including 'Thin Paper Classics' and 'The Art Library'. They were beautiful productions but totally uneconomic at the price at which they were put on sale and very costly to the company. The effect of those and similar transactions was to depress the value of the Newnes shares and to send the dividend rate down to its lowest, 2½ per cent. Sir George Newnes himself contributed an undisclosed sum to bring the profits for 1906 up to £57,000. By the next year they were down to £32,000.

He showed an old friend, Sir Grimwood Mears, a barrister who spent many years of public service in India, a letter from the Prime Minister intimating that his name was being put forward for a barony. Newnes decided to be known as Lord Wildcroft. At the Speaker's Dinner in the House of Commons he drank too freely and had to be led away. His name did not appear in the next Honours List. Sir Grimwood recalled young Frank Newnes's heartfelt cry: 'He has ruined my life!'

Lady Newnes appealed to the Rev. R. J. Campbell, of the City Temple, who was usually referred to in print as 'the noted divine', for help in trying to restore her husband's sense of responsibility to his family, his friends, and his business. The effort failed. He fell into the habit of disappearing without notice, leaving important decisions in suspense, once for six weeks.

Those were days full of difficulty for the managers of his company's affairs. They preferred to remember him, as some did gratefully, when he was the ebulliently masterful head of the great publishing edifice that he had built up from the paragraph in the provincial evening newspaper thirty years before. He had been genial, generous, and fair and, in his best moments, enheartening to work for. As one whose activities touched the lives of vast numbers of people, it could be said for him that if he did not notably elevate the general taste, neither did he use his opportunities and such power as he had to degrade it. His public spirit could not be challenged. That the name of Newnes continues to be respected throughout the publishing world must in no small measure be accorded to the integrity which he originally imparted to it.

The curtain fell on his tragedy in June 1910, at Lynton, one of the North Devon resorts whose amenities owed much to his benefactions. Flags were half-masted at many points along that coast, where the people were preparing for a new holiday season. A few months later his house there was burnt down by suffragettes. His will, made in 1895 on a sheet of foolscap, was proved after considerable delay at £174,153. That amount was swallowed up by debts to the company. Lady Newnes was to receive £3,000 a year. The bequest could not be met. Frank Newnes, still on the board of George Newnes, Limited, was put to the necessity of seeking a personal bank guarantee for £1,000 from Leicester Harmsworth, to whom he wrote on February 27, 1913: 'It helped me greatly at a difficult time.'

Lord Northcliffe (Alfred Harmsworth), whose prosperity had outsoared even his own ambitions, wrote in after years to Sir Frank Newnes: 'I knew your father very well in my early days. He was good enough to write a paragraph approving my work. I was very proud of it. I do not know what he may have become later, but in the old days in Farringdon Street he was most accessible and very kind to young people.' (May 8, 1921.)

4

Colour first appeared in *The Strand* in the years just before the First World War. To the sated modern eye it seems to have been used with nervous discretion, as if the art department had little faith in it. Tom Browne was one of the first artists to work in colour for the magazine; one of the first, also, to draw an aeroplane as an illustration for a *Strand* short story.

His versatility as an artist might have fused into genius had he not been doomed by heredity to die at 39. Connoisseurs bought his landscapes, errand-boys giggled at his comic picture postcards. As a Nottingham youth, born in 1870, he earned his first few shillings a week by delivering bonnet boxes for a local milliner. As he went about the streets of his Midland home town, he often stooped to make drawings on the pavement with a piece of chalk.

Drawing came to him as by instinct. He had no art lessons until he was twenty. He earned small sums by designing labels for cigar boxes. After serving for a time in the lithography department of a Nottingham printing house, he started a small colour printing business, Tom Browne & Co., producers of picture postcards. At 23, he left for London to draw for the new Harmsworth boys' papers. His Weary Willie and Tired Tim were 'pop' characters on a scale that would be thought vast even by today's distended standards of triumph in that line.

His health was unstable because, it was said, of his 'bad' family history. Perhaps it had relevance to his practice of working furiously for long stretches, exhausting himself in doing so. In one of his self-imposed stints he supplied five pages of drawings a week for six months without a break. He then resigned the post that guaranteed him a basic £75 a week to revert to the life of a freelance.

His work for *Punch* was an incitement to display his acutely sharp eye and ear for the humour of the bus tops and the pavements. It was often pointed humour but never malicious, a judgment supported not only by his published work but by his self-portrait, which is cherished by the Savage Club. In the gallery of black-and-white artists he has a place next to Phil May.

The flimsy aeroplane that Tom Browne drew for *The Strand* was a reminder that within the previous four years, no more, the range of human flight had been extended from ten yards to five hundred miles. Rapid advance was the story of the cinema, too. The magazine threw a beam of light into the darkness of what were still known as bioscope theatres, by revealing how film producers (not yet ranked as superior beings to directors) obtained effects that were making audiences gasp with a sense of the miraculous.

TWELVE

First World War Shadows

I

Tensions were rising on the Continent. England's island
security, inviolate for eight centuries, was being reappraised
in the light of the conquest of the air and the growth of German naval power. War talk was commonly heard at the
breakfast table, prompted by headlines about Dreadnoughts,
Zeppelins, and spies. To obtrude the personal note, I recall
(with astonishment now, having survived the two greatest
conflicts in human history), hearing a headmaster say in 1905,
pointing to Germany on a wall map of Europe: 'Some day
we shall be at war with those people.' His prophecy remained
with me, an undercurrent of dread, constantly renewed by
the speeches of belligerent politicians, rumours of large-scale
Army manoeuvres, and Jingoism in the music-halls. By 1912,
many people were resigning themselves to a woeful prospect.

The Strand Magazine deemed it timely to put the problems
of disarmament before the public, asking whether, if disarmament was practicable, it was also desirable. 'Is war an unmiti-
gated evil? Is the maintenance of gigantic armaments without
a corresponding value to the community? Able historians have
alleged indeed that war is as necessary for a high type of
civilisation as religion or literature, that it exerts an ennobling
and stimulating influence upon society. . . .' Despite its measured tone, the editorial introduction was purposely provocative.

Norman Angell, whose book, The Great Illusion, was
biblical among the partisans of peace, replied predictably that
'war would be disastrous for both England and Germany. It
would settle nothing, whichever won'. He and his friends, he
wrote, were trying 'to bring about a political reformation
that would do for the problem of useless armaments what the

intellectual reformation of the seventeenth and eighteenth centuries did for the problem of religious oppression'. With what at this distance hardly seems to have been powerful relevance, he reminded readers that Germany was 'the only considerable country in the world which has had no war for forty years'.

A new writer, W. J. Locke, author of *The Joyous Adventures of Aristide Pujol*, a series just started in the magazine, disposed of the subject with a sweeping flourish of the pen: 'Until every human being, from the Archbishop of Canterbury to the howling savage in Central Africa, is certified as a wingless angel, the total abolition of the Navy and Army would result in the abolition of society.' E. Phillips Oppenheim, whose name was to become even more familiar to *Strand* readers in the next two decades, shared the same strident certainty that 'so long as human nature remains what it is today—and during the last two thousand years it has changed remarkably little—so long will military force be the natural, wholesome, and inevitable solution of international difficulties. The nation which ceases to breed warriors and sailors will be a nation without vital impulses'. Ominous sentiments to be voiced by more ominous men in the future.

'Speaking for the great Labour Party' (to quote the unctuous editorial preface to his contribution), Ramsay MacDonald was 'absolutely convinced that the advantages of universal peace will be favourable to literature, the arts, and culture generally', his rs like Yser, rolling rapidly. 'In so far as it is necessary to stir the imagination by patriotic sentiments the historical sense will still remain to us, and will do that work in purer and brighter ways than the contemporaneous display of armies and navies. Artistic imagination would then be driven to that rich field of sheer human interest from which some of the best artistic work has received inspiration—*In Memoriam*, for instance, or Beethoven's Ninth Symphony.'

A. C. Benson, a future Cambridge college head and popular essayist, did not think that the Anglo-Saxon people would benefit much from a cultural revolution brought about by universal peace. 'Their aims have generally been too concrete and material. I should expect that a general enrichment of the country, such as would probably result from a removal of the waste inseparable from the production of the materials of war, would at first only result in an increase of bourgeois comfort.'

A diagrammatic illustration made the point that 'one year of disarmament could mean one million free allotments of garden ground of two acres apiece at £25 per acre, plus £20,000,000 for tools, seeds, etc. This would abolish starvation at once'. George Morrow, a humorous artist of later renown, proposed that Dreadnoughts should be converted into merchantmen or pleasure cruise ships, that Lord Kitchener should be appointed to 'command the railways', and that former sailors and soldiers should be recruited into a national fire-fighting force.

In the days of Queen Anne—'forsooth!'—and of George I, the small standing British army was put to roadmaking and bridge building. 'What economy, what retrenchment!' In the last ten years the nation had spent £700,000,000 on armaments. 'Peace, once the cheapest of commitments, has grown into a most expensive one.'

The dilemma deepened the national self-consciousness, which was manifest again in an article that had for its title: *Is England On The Down-Grade?* Beset by his newly assumed responsibilities as First Lord of the Admiralty, Winston Churchill appeared to be only half attentive to the implications of the question. 'There is no chance whatever of our being overtaken in naval strength unless we want to be. We think that we can build as well and as good ships as any other constructors in the world. I could put it higher, but, as Dr Johnson observes, "On their own merits modest men are dumb." '

American-born Sir Hiram Maxim, inventor of the machine-gun, believed that if England were governed 'by a class of men who thought more of their country than of their political party, and had sufficient backbone to see that the laws were rigidly executed', she would 'make greater progress than any other country in the world'. The foremost boxing referee, Eugene Corri, conceded that English boxers 'have certainly not improved within recent years. As the mother of boxing,

England latterly has not turned out such skilful and sturdy children as she did a decade or so ago. 'Peggy' Bettinson, Tom Hill, Bob Hare, John Douglas, and the Dearsleys represented a better-class brand of boxer than the majority of the best-known exponents of the fistic art today'.

A Lancashire cotton magnate, Sir Charles Macara, had 'never known public spirit in England to be at a lower ebb'. He attributed it to 'the absorbing interest in party politics to which everything else appears to be subservient'. Sir Joseph Lyons, of teashop fame, responded in terms that the statesmen did not formulate until much later and, as is now evident, to our cost:

'The population of the world increases in a ratio which is not met by a commensurate increase in the supplies from the land for that ever-growing mass of humanity. It would help a great deal if more British capital were put into some of our Colonies for the production of foodstuffs, making those Colonies more prosperous and rendering the Mother Country less dependent upon foreign nations. I am no specialist in world troubles, but I think my way would reduce inflammation.'

Academic innuendos from Germany on England's alleged decline gave the subject obsessive significance in those last months of peace. *Have Undergraduates Deteriorated?* evoked the views of Dr Warren, of Magdalen College, Oxford, the Rev. W. M. Spooner, Fellow and Tutor of New College, Oxford, the Warden of Wadham College, Oxford, the Principal of University College, Oxford, the Master of Magdalene, Cambridge, the Master of Clare College, Cambridge, the Vice-Chancellor of the University of Cambridge, and the Master of King's College, Cambridge. 'The consensus of opinion would seem to be that the average undergraduate both physically, intellectually, and morally is a better man than his predecessor of twenty or thirty years ago. We can therefore rest in the hope that the ancient universities, nurses of so many famous Englishmen, may for many years continue the good work for Church and State.'

As if in a placatory mood, the magazine announced 'an article of special interest and importance' with the intimidating title: *The Kaiser As He Is*. It might have been purposely devised to allay anxiety in the chancelleries. There was the courtly introduction: 'The following article has been written by one who is in intimate personal contact with the German emperor, and has been specially approved by his Imperial Majesty. This is the first occasion upon which permission for such an article to be published has been granted by the Kaiser to any British magazine.' Was it a reverberating effect of George Newnes's success in securing the personal interest in his magazine of Queen Victoria, the Kaiser's grandmother? *The Strand* had always been favourably regarded in royal circles.

The 'interest and importance' of the article evaporated all too soon, leaving only the echo of its pathetic fallacy that there was hope for the future in 'a moving little incident' that occurred when the Kaiser was in London in May 1913 for the unveiling of the National Memorial to Queen Victoria. After the ceremony, 'he was seen to draw the arm of King George through his own in the most affectionate fashion. One could not help considering the meaning of their earnest conversation, and how far it contributed to the peace of Europe'.

2

The Argentine tango was the rage of the dance floor. Phyllis Dare wrote an instructional article about it for *The Strand*. The magazine plumed itself on the success of its Charles Dickens Birth Centenary Appeal Fund, which 'places his five granddaughters, Mary, Evelyn, Ethel, Dorothy and Cecil, for ever out of the reach of want. Their patience and pluck in adversity are known to all'.

They were the daughters of Dickens's eldest son. Among the papers relating to *The Strand Magazine* appeal was a copy, marked 'Private', of a letter written from 15 Cliffords Inn, Fleet Street, by the eldest of the granddaughters, Ethel, to their uncle Henry, the novelist's youngest son, later Sir Henry Dickens, K.C. He had made a statement to the *Daily Telegraph* in March 1911 declaring that 'the Dickens family are not in necessitous circumstances', as was suggested by the organisers of the fund.

'Dear Uncle Henry', Ethel Dickens wrote on March 20. 'Evelyn and Dolly (both of whom are not at all strong or fit for work at all) are just barely making a living, and Cecil is one of the Secretaries to the National Health Society at a salary of £110 per annum.' Ethel Dickens herself was in the doctor's hands. 'He tells me that nothing but six months' rest is the least use to me.' Objecting to her uncle's declaration, she added: 'We have none of us been able to make enough money to save. Poverty through absolutely no fault of one's own cannot possibly be regarded as a disgrace, and I am absolutely sure that my Grandfather himself would not, were he now alive, be ashamed of us and of our acknowledgment of our pecuniary position.'

She questioned whether she should contradict her uncle in print. 'It does not appear to me quite seemly.' On March 21, the *Daily Telegraph* published a letter from Henry Dickens regretting that he had 'used language that gave a contrary impression'.

Ethel Dickens ran a typewriting bureau in Wellington Street, Strand. A large display board on the front wall announced: 'MISS DICKENS—TYPEWRITING.' She typed many of Shaw's plays and did other work for him.

The serialisation of extracts from Captain Scott's journals, recovered from the burial tent in the Antarctic, was the magazine coup of 1913; price, £2,000. The last poignant photographs were splendidly reproduced.

The first aerial combats in history had yet to be fought. In the January 1914 issue a glimpse of what might portend was given in a short story that envisaged air warfare being conducted on the play-the-game principles of British sportsmanship. The illustrator's concept of a duel in space was realised in line-and-wash drawings that would have not been amiss in a schoolboys' magazine. Otherwise that year of fate for mankind cast no grim warning shadows across the pages of *The Strand*.

On the contrary, the magazine was at the high peak of its prosperity. It was 'bulked out' with 110 pages of advertising, into which colour had just been introduced, its first users Cherry Blossom Boot Polish; Sanatogen, 'The Tonic-Food'; O. K. Sauce.

Editorially, the advent of a glamorous new race of beings was celebrated in *Stories of the Film Stars*, who smirked out of sepia half-tones that indicated a new impetus in the art department. At last, *The Strand* condescended to recognise Wardour Street, whose minions had long haunted the offices of *Tit-Bits* on the next floor. Now Alma Taylor, Chrissie White, Blanche Sweete, Anna Nilsson, Alice Joyce, Gabrielle Robinne, and Marie Pickering were presented as 'high goddesses of the newest and most thrustful branch of the entertainment industry in England. In the accompanying text the cinema was still referred to as the biograph theatre.

Gladys Cooper Tells Her Story was another sign of Greenhough Smith's editorial imperturbability. He was himself writing an article on the remote subject of Tamerlane for inclusion in a series called Real Life Romances. Its first sentence was 168 words long, expertly punctuated. He broke new ground with articles on women's fashions by men who knew nothing about them and who wrote the more entertainingly because of it. His chief contributor in that line was a briskly energetic, ruthless little man named Gordon Meggy, of an Essex local newspaper-owning family, who had been one of Northcliffe's young men until he was fired for playing billiards in Fleet Street at 11 a.m. He started The Premier School of Journalism, his sole capital twenty-five shillings taken from a child's money-box (the price of an advertisement in the Personal Column of *The Times*), plus considerable nerve, and his file of *Strand Magazine* articles, impressively bound, with which to dazzle prospective pupils. A recent prospectus of the School named him with 'Lawrence' (for Laurence) Housman and George Bernard Shaw as the 'three great writers' who influenced its fortunes. It would appear that the founder's nerve is still potent in that quarter.

No war topics are listed under W in *The Strand Magazine* index for 1914. *Portraits of Celebrities* included Lord Kitchener and Reginald McKenna, who was to be a wartime Chancellor of the Exchequer. *Illustrated Interviews*, that once irresistible series, had been displaced by *Reminiscences*, in which noted men and women discoursed to the extent of several pages on early phases of their careers. The semi-mythical 'Joe' Lyons, of the far-flung catering dynasty bearing his name, surprised many by revealing that he meant to make a living by art and that he had exhibited at the Royal Institute of British Artists, where he found buyers for his pictures. Two of them were reproduced in the magazine. For Arnold Bennett, it was a chance to recall piquant incidents of his Paris period and to refute the legend of his being a man 'who always does what he says he will do'.

For a reason not now obvious, the magazine reverted to its original practice of publishing short stories translated from foreign sources, chiefly French and Russian. It cannot have been from a want of native talent or that it was necessarily more strenuously engaged. Perceval Gibbon, the ex-merchant seaman of uncertain temper who aspired to rival his friend Conrad and whose work often produced the reaction: 'How good this would be if only it were a little better'; Stacy Aumonier, whose short story titles still echo in the mind: *The Octave of Jealousy, Where is Wych Street? Miss Brace-girdle Does Her Duty*; Roland Pertwee, another in the top flight of short-story competence; Keble Howard (J. Keble Bell), who resigned the editorship of *The Sketch* for the less blinkered reputation of a fiction writer; F. Britten Austin, the large earnings of whose busy and vivid pen were not large enough to sustain him in his last years; Stephen McKenna who wrote *Sonia*, one of the few notable novels to appear during the First World War—all were zestful and valued contributors to *The Strand* from the year 1917 onward.

Looking over the records, one finds weathercock variations in price. An O. Henry short story, *The Cop and the Anthem*, was marked up at £10, a P. G. Wodehouse story at £40: he had just introduced Jeeves to *The Strand* public. Britten Austin was paid £31 10s, Roland Pertwee £21 10s. Towering loftily above them was A. E. W. Mason, at £166 13s 4d a story. W. W. Jacobs's price had bounded from £240 to £350.

3

As *The Strand* went to press five weeks ahead of publication, the happenings of July and August 1914 had no effect on those months' issues. The August number opened with a military short story called *The Ranker*, by Frank Verney. It showed no prescience of events. Mess jackets were a feature of the illustrations. *How to Improve Your Batting By Fifty Per Cent*, an article by J. Hobbs, the Surrey professional, presumably failed of its purpose, for by the time it appeared most of the nation's cricketing amateurs had joined in the rush to the recruiting offices.

The first article with a war theme was *Our Friends the Fighting Rajahs* (December 1914), which lauded, praised, and probably magnified the services of the Indian princes to the Allied cause. It was given prominence also in the American edition (published at 83-85 Duane Street, New York City), for which Sir Arthur Conan Doyle wrote *A Statement of The British Case*, filling eight pages of the same issue.

One could believe that American subscribers were more readily diverted by *How I Broke Into Print* by Irvin Cobb, Elbert Hubbard, Montague Glass, Louis Joseph Vance, and Richard Washburn Child, the last-named claiming that 'authorship is one part writing and nine parts breathless wonder'. In any case, the American *Strand* was soon to be closed down. There were years in which it paid its way. It never made money for the Newnes firm and rising war costs finally eclipsed its chances of doing so.[1]

Our Greatest Victories on Sea and Land, in 1915, summoned past glories at a time when inglorious stalemate had come to the opposing armies stretched out along a line of four hundred miles from the Swiss marches to the Straits of Dover. Admirals and generals on the retired list, war historians, military critics, cast votes that produced a 'top twelve' result: at sea, Trafalgar, The Nile, Defeat of the Spanish Armada, Quiberon, St Vincent, Camperdown; on land, Waterloo, Salamanca, Blenheim, Plassey, Quebec, Crécy-Agincourt. The illustrations, taken from famous battle pieces, were sufficiently graphic. Men beleaguered in Flanders mud may not have felt the surge of pride. The we'll-show-'em spirit was possibly stiffened in the Service clubs, where *The Strand* was always popular reading.

[1] The American edition ceased publication in 1916.

Among the public men singled out for notice in the magazine at that stage of the world crisis was Winston Churchill, then aged 40, of whom it was noted, surprisingly, that 'his face bears evidence of much mental work and responsibility'. A Churchill that a later generation would hardly recognise. 'He already wears spectacles for reading and writing.' To the writer of the article, 'he is a singular combination of youthfulness and age'. A familiar charge is repeated: 'He has the defects of his qualities. He sometimes acts too much on the impulse of the moment.'

THIRTEEN

Conan Doyle and the Fairies

I

In 1916 *The Strand* came out with the bold-type question: *Is The Kaiser Mad?* To some readers who remembered the respectful article on the German emperor only three or four years earlier it seemed a lapse of editorial responsibility that he should be arraigned in the crude propagandist spirit of the hour. Not all were mollified by the co-operation of the 'eminent brain experts' who were invited to give their opinions.

The experts were Dr R. Armstrong-Jones, 'well-known as Resident Physician and Superintendent of the L.C.C. Asylum, Claybury', Dr T. B. Hyslop, formerly Superintendent of Bedlam, and Dr Morton Prince, 'a highly reputed psychologist'. Their diagnosis was no doubt a popular one, their recommendation in effect: 'An asylum—or St Helena.' It can but have exacerbated the feelings of those who resented the exposure of a direct descendant of Queen Victoria, whatever his personal defects, to the indignity of such an inquiry.

That year the circulation department had cause to revise its faith in the pulling power of a famous name. The magazine extensively advertised its satisfaction in having 'acquired the exclusive rights' (for £5,000) in Sir Arthur Conan Doyle's *History of the British Campaign in France and Flanders*. He toiled manfully to keep abreast of events as they occurred. His narrative power was fully stretched through nineteen instalments. There was every sign of his having relished a task that would have been a heavy one for a man of more youthful energy. The public did not respond in any important sense.

Conan Doyle's claim that his information throughout was 'particularly good' failed to impress the military critics when they came to review the work in volume form. It was felt with considerable unanimity that he had not distinguished himself as a war historian. 'I would reckon it the greatest and most undeserved literary disappointment of my life', he later wrote in *Memories and Adventures*, while proclaiming his belief that posterity would form a more favourable judgment. Perhaps there was some slight consolation for him, after all, in an article written for *The Strand* by E. E. Stevenson, a public librarian, who reported that 'Sherlock Holmes is still the supreme fiction detective'.

It was an imaginative idea to reprint H. G. Wells's short story, *The Land Ironclads*, shortly after the first tanks had appeared like elephantine apparitions out of the mists of the Somme Valley. The story had originally been published in the magazine thirteen years earlier, in 1903. It was hailed editorially in 1916 as 'a prophecy fulfilled, the most startling case on record in which the vision of a fiction writer has "come true" in actual fact'.

The suggestion that England's remarkable new secret weapon owed anything to Wells's foresight was discounted in the magazine by Colonel E. D. Swinton, who was concerned with the project from the drawing-board stage. According to him, the evolution of the tank was founded on an engineering principle first applied to agricultural machinery in 1914 by an American named Holt at Peoria, Illinois. As for the name, it was 'part of the strategy of surprise'.

The explanation did not satisfy F. J. Gardiner, Fellow of the Royal Historical Society, who informed *The Strand* that the term 'tank' was taken from the name of Thomas Tank Burall, manager of the Thetford Engineering Works, Norfolk, who, long before 1914, designed a caterpillar track device to be fitted to traction-engines moving over rough ground. Tank was his mother's maiden name.

It was not referred to in the 'full story' of the genesis of the new weapon written exclusively for *The Strand* after the war by Sir Albert Stern, R.N.V.R., who took part in the secret conferences on its production held at the White Hart, Lincoln. He gave the possibly relevant information that the first tank crews were trained at Thetford.

2

Paper imports were reduced to two-thirds, then to one-half, of the pre-war supplies. Although there was some falling away of advertising, it was not found necessary to make a cut in the number of pages in *The Strand* up to 1917, nor was there any change in the page size. As the submarine campaign intensified that year, a thinner magazine became inevitable. A smaller body type was used. The rule of 'a picture on every page' was dropped, and with it colour printing, 'for the duration'. The circulation was pegged at the half-million mark. Demand still exceeded it.

Wartime readers wanted diversion from the overriding theme. The editorial policy was re-defined with the accent on entertainment. Charlie Chaplin was elevated to the dignity of *Portraits of Celebrities* . . . . in the company of Lord Rhondda, the Food Minister, who would have been startled to know that he was a subject of spicy disclosures made by 'the little Canadian adventurer', Max Aitken (later Lord Beaverbrook) to his friend Arnold Bennett, who wrote them down in his notebooks as material for a novel.

Sherlock Holmes, foiling the machinations of a German villain named Von Bork, greeted his medical companion with unwonted warmth. 'Good old Watson! You are the one fixed point in a changing age.' He saw tribulation ahead. 'There's an east wind coming . . . such a wind as never blew on England yet.'[1]

At that point, *The Strand* appears to have decided that humour was the anodyne, that it was part of its patriotic duty to support and illustrate the statement of Rudyard Kipling, newly returned from a tour of the Western Front, that the English were 'the only genuinely humorous race on earth'. Thereafter, every issue contained an article on some aspect of humour, mostly centred in the work of leading humorous artists: H. M. Bateman, master of the subtle *contretemps*; Heath Robinson, who anticipated, with his own fluent inventiveness, the mechanical eccentricities of Rowland Emett; G. L. Stampa, long endeared to *Punch* readers

[1] *The Last Bow: The War Service of Sherlock Holmes* (1917).

by his urchin drawings; George Belcher, who made Mrs Mopp a public character years before she was typified by that name; Bert Thomas, whose '*Arf a Mo*', *Kaiser* was one of the comic cartoon successes of the war; Lawson Wood, whose rollicking pencil endowed the most sluggish animal subject with weird animation.

The scope was infinitely wide: golf humour, prison humour, humours of hospital life, of the Scottish bench and bar, even the humour of the chemist's shop, from which it was obvious that the influence of the music-hall was not yet dead in the land. 'So you've forgotten what you came for?' 'Ah that's it—camphor! What does it sulphur?' 'I've never cinnamon so funny!' 'Never mind me, ammonia novice.' Many of the jokes quoted were indeed little more than patter picked up over the footlights.

Taking Kipling's statement for his text, a thesis writer might not have found it easy to sustain the argument from those numbers of *The Strand* of the First World War. Captain Bruce Bairnsfather's mittened Old Bill, crouching over his brazier, or peering above the trench to complain: 'There goes our blinkin' parapet again', already seemed an antediluvian figure to the men of the New Army, whose humour was more sophisticated, if still answerable to the sanctions of a conventional society.

As for the sense of humour, concerning which Englishmen tended to behave as if they held the world copyright, apparently acquired when *Punch* was started in the 1840s, where in the kingdom was it most convincingly manifested? The question was a typical one for *The Strand*, which continued to overwork the symposium technique of eliciting the views of people with 'names'. On that occasion, the contributors were famous comedians.

Three of them gave the palm to London: George Formby, senior, Alfred Lester, and Little Tich (who specified the West End). Harry Tate split his vote between Yorkshire and 'the real Cockneys'. G. P. Huntley's choice was Glasgow, Nelson Keys' was Cambridge. It was not a particularly enlightening inquiry into the nation's risible responses.

The note of controversy was pitched in a higher key with

the serialisation of Mrs Asquith's autobiography, a work of zestful indiscretion that helped to create a climate favourable to the new era of biographical irreverence. American magazines, headed by the *Saturday Evening Post*, were back in the British market. *The Strand* had laurels to look to. Its serial publication of the exploits of Lawrence of Arabia was another sign of renewed editorial vigour.

Familiar initials vanished from the art side, 'S. P.' (Sidney Paget), 'A. P.' (Alfred Pearse), and with them the signatures of H. R. Millar, Gordon Browne, A. Forestier, Paul Hardy. More contemporary illustrators stepped into their shoes: Lewis Baumer, Stephen Spurrier, G. E. Studdy, Nora Schlegel, Arthur Watts, A. K. Macdonald, L. G. Illingworth, Alfred Sindall, Gilbert Wilkinson, Gordon Nicoll. Colour work was resumed. The new artists were paired off with the new story writers, Edgar Wallace, 'Bartimeus', Lynn Doyle, Gilbert Frankau, 'Sapper'.

3

Edgar Wallace wrote for the magazine a new series of his *Four Just Men* stories (seen by the television millions in dramatised form in the 1960s). He had published the first batch under that title at his own expense several years before the war, probably emboldened by the example of Hall Caine, who financed the publication of his own novels—one of them, *The Eternal City* (1901), sold a million copies—at great personal profit. Wallace's experiment was disastrous. He incurred a loss that would have forced him into bankruptcy but for the last-hour intervention of Lord Northcliffe, his employer at the time. Wallace's letter of gratitude was almost abject. In due course, needing ready money again, he sold the original series outright to Newnes for £75 and had the mortification of seeing the sales soar at no further benefit to himself. His fortunes took a better turn with the publication of his *Sanders of the River* stories. They proved that his racily omniscient style could command the attention of a large public.

The swifter movement of postwar life encouraged the

legend of Wallace's phenomenal dexterity as a writer. It was overplayed, not unwarranted. The *Daily Express* asked him by telephone how soon he could deliver the first instalment of a serial story urgently required to back the circulation drive towards its second million. He answered: 'In four days.' It was Thursday. The price was agreed at £2,250, half in advance, the length at 'not less than eighty thousand words'. A title was proposed to him, *The Man from the Carlton*. It was given lavish publicity before a word of the story had been written. The opening chapter was on the literary editor's desk by the following Sunday afternoon. It appeared in the next morning's issue and from then on the story proceeded smoothly to its appointed end.

At devising new situations in the realm of crime, detection, and the underworld in general, including the murkier parts of the Turf, Wallace was a master hand. Plots sprang up at a wave of his ridiculously long cigarette holder. Character was another thing; his invention often failed him there, with exceptions such as the gangster Pirelli in *On The Spot*. What mattered to his readers, who became legion, was not only that he could tell a story, but that he always had a story to tell. Recording that of the 14,399 books published in the United Kingdom in 1928 no fewer than 81 were by Edgar Wallace, the *London Mercury* proposed the appointment of 'a Dr Marie Stopes of Literature'.

It fell to me to have various dealings with him when he was at the peak of a fame that eclipsed Conan Doyle's with the new reading public. Here I can insert a pertinent parenthesis. At a preparatory school fathers' match I was asked by a small boy for my autograph. 'Why *my* autograph?' I inquired, it being the first request of the kind ever addressed to me. The answer came pat: 'Please, sir, it's because you know Edgar Wallace.' I invited Wallace to join some other well-known writers in an autobiographical series that was being prepared for publication under the unequivocal title of *Who I Am*. He telephoned his regret. 'You see, old cock, I'm a bastard.'

As a child, he was abandoned on a doorstep in Billingsgate, where he was brought up by a fish porter's wife. As a man, he never behaved as if he had any bitterness of soul on that account. Doubtless those early circumstances supplied drives that carried him well past prudence in certain of his business affairs. They did not inhibit the development in him of like-able qualities, including imperturbable serenity between displays of flashy conceit.

His intelligence was largely acquisitive, understandably so. He never got the better of his gambling instinct. There were softening elements in his nature. He had an ear for good poetry. He was warm-hearted, tolerant, and wittily amusing. He had friends in every walk of life and he was the same man to them all.

When he died in Hollywood in 1932, *The Times* honoured him in a leading article. It was a more fitting memorial than the assertively high marble cross put over his grave in the cemetery at Little Marlow.

4

Peter Jackson, Cigar Merchant, was one of the first war novels to lay bare the miseries of the neurasthenia that darkened the lives of many demobilised young officers facing readjustment to civilian life. Its author, Gilbert Frankau, was himself a victim, one of many who resorted to the consulting-room at 132 Harley Street of Laughton Scott, senior physician of the London Neurological Clinic, who worked devotedly to relieve the abounding mental distress of that time.

As Frankau's mother was the once well-known novelist who wrote as 'Frank Danby', presumably he inherited her fluent story-telling gift. He was capable of applying it with the calculating efficiency of one who is adamant about catching the 9.15. No ardent self-deceiver, he was also capable of calling his own bluff. He had an incisive humour that atoned for his tendency to social aggressiveness. He lived most of his time at full tilt and could not see that a source of difficulty for him was his refusal to recognise his intellectual limitations, which were severe. Hence, for example, his right-wing Tory bitterness against intellectuals. His frequent attacks on them were all sound and fury.

His first *Strand* stories, collected under the title of *Men,*

Maids and Mustard Pot, were written out of his hunting field experiences, from which he had hoped for restorative balm for his war-shattered nerves. They placed him well below the narrative masters whose work was familiar in those pages. When a critic generously assigned him to the second rank, Frankau took it as a disappointing compliment.

As a writer, who had begun by passably emulating Byron's *Don Juan*, he had nothing to offer posterity except an inventory of period moods: dancing to the music of the Savoy Orpheans, horseback dialogues, 'corkscrewing down to Monte Carlo' in fast Italian cars, cocktails at the Berkeley, and after-dinner repartee over mahogany and old silver. He could pare a love scene down to a few not particularly well-chosen words: 'Then his eyes shone at her and his arms took her to him', the kind of thing that made Greenhough Smith say to Horace Annesley Vachell, another of the *Strand* authors: 'You know, Vachell, as an editor I have to scrap my own tastes. Personally, I dislike the stories which I know will please the many.'

For myself, I enjoyed Frankau's company and valued his sense of obligation as a friend. There was an afternoon at Hove in the last months of his life, he having offered to give me 'a story or two' for the biography of Arnold Bennett. No one could have been more readily helpful with advice, information, and suggestions. He had a strong antipathy, I remember, to footnotes. During our walk on the Lawns he halted to take tablets for his heart condition. He was unduly concerned (I thought) to discover Jewish affinities in a publisher known to us both. What importance it had for him at that time of his fast-failing strength was not clear.

In 1933, he astonished his friends, and pained many other people, by writing, at his own suggestion, an article for the *Daily Express* under the heading: *As A Jew, I Am Not Against Hitler*. For a few who remembered his mother's novel, *Pigs in Clover*, it was like the echo of an old defiance. Herself a Jewess, she affronted the Jewish community by her bitter portrayal of types of Jew to be found in English society. The American edition of the novel disappeared from public view soon after its publication there; according to the book trade, it was suppressed by conspiratorial design.

I remember mentioning to Frankau, as we walked the Hove Lawns, that one of his co-religionists, R. D. Blumenfeld, for forty years editor of the *Daily Express*, had recently. in an intense upsurge of ancestral emotion, returned to the faith of their forefathers and wholeheartedly embraced Zionism. Frankau showed no interest. It transpired that he was contemplating quite a different step. Nearing his end, he was received into the Roman Catholic Church.

He had charm, wit, gaiety of heart, and independence of spirit. It may not have been unfairly construed as foolhardiness when he wrote in *The Strand* that he 'loathed democracy and all the ways thereof'.

5

'Sapper' (H. C. McNeile) was a young officer of the Royal Engineers, of Scottish descent from Belfast, who at first turned to writing as a means of defeating the tedium of trench life on the Western Front. Scribbling his way through a succession of notebooks, he was no fevered aspirant to literary distinction. For the time being, all that he wanted was mental relief.

The outcome was *Sergeant Michael Cassidy* and encouragement from *The Strand Magazine;* then *Bulldog Drummond* and no looking back, his fortune made from the hackneyed device of an imaginary Personal Column 'ad' in the *Morning Post* (then the paper for 'top people'): 'Demobilised officer, finding peace incredibly tedious, would welcome diversion . . . Excitement essential . . . Reply at once Box X10.' Preposterously English, Drummond was born to lead and to chastise, whether with rhinoceros hide whip, fists, the toe of his riding boot, or a revolver.

He was not so fastidious about firearms as James Bond, who gave considerable substance to his shadow forty years on. He was not less violent in enmity, and his adversaries were as tough and as evil as any depicted by Ian Fleming, who conceivably would have approved his taste in young women. Whereas one is rarely tempted to laugh at Bond, some of

Drummond's reactions invite jeers, an effect not lessened by Sir Gerald Du Maurier's stiff-jawed stage personification, with his cigarette flourish and his mannered restraint.

'Sapper' told *The Strand* how Drummond and his chief enemy were evolved. 'Troubles over demobilisation were rife; men were discontented; the soil was ripe for agitators. Believing firmly as I do that 90% of agitators are concerned with their own pockets, and care no whit for their wretched dupes . . . I decided to make Carl Peterson an Arch-Communist.' Drummond was conceived as the executive head of 'a society for the extermination of unpleasing individuals'.

Bond was the more rounded character, and the more feasible, because he came from the imagination of a mature man. Drummond never grew up and that may not be an unfair verdict on his master. 'Sapper' was dead before fifty, outlasting only by a year Rudyard Kipling, who shaped his prejudices and confirmed him in his prefect's attitude to his fellow-men.

6

England a land fit for heroes to live in: it was one of the slogans of victory. Even so, it is surprising to find in *The Strand* an article on *How Much Land Does A Man Want?* by Tolstoy. The effect is a little like that of a driver loosening the reins to a stampeding horse. Nor is a sense of stability recovered by the discussions of the life-after-death theme, no doubt thought timely when so many homes had suffered bereavement, and possibly initiated in deference to the view of Conan Doyle, still the magazine's most influential contributor.

He speaks affirmatively to the question: *Is Sir Oliver Lodge Right?* The negative line is taken by Edward Clodd, the banker, poet, and Rationalist. Readers learn that Sir Oliver was a psychic investigator long before the death of his son Raymond, which inspired his celebrated book of that name. Conan Doyle insists that there are 'grades of living beyond our dimension. We are like the fish in the Kentucky lakes and see not'.

Shaw and Wells join in refuting Doyle and Lodge. Wells dismisses the argument with the assertion that 'the whole idea of a *personal* immortality is absurd on the face of it'. Shaw quotes Dean Inge, 'a brilliant man. I agree with what he says in one of his Outspoken Essays. He points out that belief in immortality depends on faith in supra-temporal absolute values; which brings us to an order of ideas which has nothing in common with the "revelations" on which spiritualists base their beliefs'.

Conan Doyle amplifies his opinions in a 'special interview' given to *The Strand*. In the course of it he refers to thirty mothers known to him who are communicating with their sons killed in the war. 'In only two cases has there been absolute failure.' He is so convinced of the truth of his findings that he refuses to accept fees for lecturing on them.

The credulity of possibly an embarrassing number of readers was tested by the main feature of the Christmas Number for 1921 '*Fairies Photographed: An Epoch-Making Event.*' How much persuasion Doyle brought to bear on Greenhough Smith to publish it was not a matter of office record. 'Should the incidents here narrated, and the photographs attached, hold their own against the criticism which they will excite, it is no exaggeration to say that they will mark an epoch in human thought.'

Conan Doyle's endorsement of the photographs, which showed two unnamed Yorkshire schoolgirls watching fairies in a grassy dell near their home at Cottingley, was supported by a Theosophist, Edward L. Gardner, of 5 Craven Road, Harlesden, N.W., and by a photographic expert named Snelling, of 26 The Bridge, Wealdstone, Harrow. The pictures, which were taken 'at 3 p.m. on a brilliantly hot and sunny day at a distance of 4ft', were submitted for examination by Kodak, Ltd., 'who could find no flaw'.[1] Conan Doyle wrote: 'I have no reason to doubt the veracity of the girls. Why should we be so cocksure that we are the only inhabitants on this material plane? More especially in these days of

---

[1] The 'Cottingley Fairies' were discussed in the *Journal of the Society for Psychical Research*, Jan.-Feb., 1946 and in the *International Journal of Parapsychology*, Winter 1965.

"wireless'. is it not time that our vision was extended to include the existence of beings nearer it may be to the heart of Nature than we are ourselves?'

For most readers that was 'voyaging on strange seas of thought'. They recoiled by making fun of Conan Doyle's latest psychic obsession. The hints grew louder that he was unbalanced by his researches. He developed his two *Strand* articles about the fairy photographs into a book. It did nothing to repair the shaken confidence of old admirers, whose scepticism was not arrested by the supporting testimony of a new *Strand* author, H. de Vere Stacpoole, who was a believer in 'the little people'. Like Doyle, he was of Irish descent and, as the author of *The Blue Lagoon*, was regarded as being susceptible to romantic fancies.

There had been misgivings at Newnes about the reiterated emphasis on spiritualism in the magazine. Advertisers preferred that readers should be preoccupied by the things of this world. Greenhough Smith tried to steer Conan Doyle away from the subject. Doyle told him: 'I wish I could do as you wish, but, as you know, my life is dedicated to one end at present. I can only write what comes to me.'

Good Looks in Men: What Types Do Women Like Best?— the editorial feet were firmly on the ground again. Mrs Belloc Lowndes replied that 'the average woman certainly prefers instinctively a manly, powerful-looking man—and that whether he be plain or handsome in face'. May Edginton did not doubt that 'in her inmost heart a woman prefers a face which denotes physical strength'. Her prime example was the boxer Jim Corbett. Clare Sheridan chose Shelley—'a tremendous character; so frank with himself, so idealistic and democratic. I would like to have been his wife'.

Mrs Baillie Reynolds agreed that 'with most of us looks are a factor in the choice made, but not mere animal good looks. A healthy physique, a good expression, an intelligent forehead, or a sweet-tempered mouth, are the things that weigh'. The Baroness Orczy, author of *The Scarlet Pimpernel*, counselled readers to 'seek for the humorous lines around the lips, for the humorous twinkle in the eyes, and trust that face more than you would that of the Adonis or the Hercules'. For her the manly ideal was represented by Lord Leighton, R.A. The ladies gave a majority of votes for Lord Kitchener, whose biography would show that he was no ladies' man.

FOURTEEN

Farewell to Sherlock Holmes

I

Those were 'the dancing years', the 1920s. Flippancy was the highest note in the social harmonics. Only faint echoes of it were recorded in *The Strand*, mostly in the anthologies of contemporary humour which the magazine was publishing during that period of intermittent confusion at home and abroad, when more than once it seemed that chaos must come again.

The services of a specialist in topical humour were acquired. He was Fenn Sherie, son of the new art editor, a talented freelance who wrote scripts for some of the reigning 'comics' of the stage and screen, among them, later on, Sid Fields and Vic Oliver. His sedulously compiled collections show that the prevailing tone of the people's humour was still warm and kindly, still preoccupied with the minor domestic misfortunes, like housemaid's knee, and shortsightedness, and with nervous curates, tipsy revellers, and mothers-in-law. Much of it was inane, hardly any of it satirical or cruel. The editorial attitude was entirely uncritical. Theories of laughter, the analytical views of Bergson and Havelock Ellis, were irrelevant. The guiding principle was that of Traddles: 'Nothing scientific.'

Just off the south side of the Strand, within a stone's throw of the office, a vastly important development in social evolution was being organised, one that would decisively affect public attitudes, tastes, and habits. For the moment it was known by the cryptic formula 2LO, the call sign of the new British broadcasting service. 'Wireless' was not yet 'radio', even at sea where it was some way past the experimental phase. Its imminence on land was forecast in an article affirming that 'wireless is now within the reach of everyone'. Cat's-whisker tuning was soon to be replaced by the new valve sets.

The Strand stressed that 'a good receiver gives out every note with perfect clearness and excellent tone, especially if the headphones are used. The loud-speaking attachment, though it answers well for orchestral pieces and will often give quite good results for instrumental solos, is still not capable of bringing out the full beauty of the master-singer's golden notes'.

Predictably, inevitably almost, there followed an article on 'the humours of wireless', illustrated by drawings from *Punch* and other sources. An elderly lady passenger on a liner was shown standing expectantly beside a huge deck ventilator and asking a passing officer: 'Can you tell me when the wireless concert commences?' The timing was as right as the smiles were broad. The loudspeaker was about to become a household appliance.

Advancing technology had introduced a new colloquialism into the popular vocabulary, 'the mike'. *The Strand* quoted the experiences of public men as first-time broadcasters. Sir Gerald Du Maurier, the actor, had recently been initiated into microphone techniques. 'I thought the whole thing was an elaborate and stupid joke.' Seymour Hicks, not yet a stage knight, was 'not nervous of the instrument itself but of the party of expert announcers who sat in the studio, listening to me'. Sir Henry Wood, of Promenade Concerts fame, thought that 'the mike' was already having a beneficial effect on musical performances.

Sir Oliver Lodge was thoroughly at ease when confronting it, a medium through which he 'had fascinated listeners by his talks on the infinitely little—the protons and electrons which, as compared with the atom, are as a dew moth in St Paul's Cathedral'. His solemn reference to 'the unsearchable Mind who is at home in infinity' had made a great impression on the still small but fast-growing listening audience.

2

Otherwise, *The Strand* proceeded sedately on its course through a decade of social frivolity, economic turmoil, depressing Budgets, political strife. It had nothing to say about the 'new poor', the decline of the larger country houses, the financial scandals, the General Strike, or the war debts that bedevilled Anglo-American relations. Nor did the menacing shadow of Ireland fall across Southampton Street, though its gunmen had been active elsewhere in London.

The undisturbed editorial urbanity was typified by *Perplexities*, the monthly puzzle feature that had been running unbrokenly for sixteen years under the name of Henry E. Dudeney. Earlier, he had contributed to the magazine as 'Sphinx', a pseudonym which he brought with him from *Tit-Bits*, the original market for his ingenious talent. He appears to have been the first man to make puzzle solving a profession. As a young Civil Servant, he had time to indulge an interest that was furthered by his success in deciphering a code message in the 'agony column' of a newspaper. From then on, solving and inventing puzzles was his chief preoccupation. Perhaps a genetic principle was at work. He was a collateral descendant of an ancient prodigy of the South Downs, John Dudeney, the Sussex shepherd-mathematician.

Henry Dudeney spent most of his years at Castle House, Lewes, where his wife wrote novels that were more than locally esteemed. Tall, bearded, ancestral-looking, he was akin to his forebear of the Downs in his preference for the solitary life. He was content to pass his days in his book-lined study, pondering the mysteries of number and magnitude, devising new problems, and adapting old ones, for readers of *The Strand*. They wrote to him from all parts of the world. Many of his most regular correspondents were long-term hospital patients. For his highly specialised labours he was paid ten guineas a month.

He was asked by the editor which mathematical problem had proved the hardest to solve in his experience. He said that he had been 'baffled for a long time' by a proposition that required him to seat thirteen people round a table on thirty-six occasions, 'so that no person should have the same two neighbours twice'. He had spent months in 'worrying it out'. It was while he was listening to a performance of *Siegfried* that a possible solution presented itself. 'I made a rough note in the margin of the programme. The next day I settled down afresh to the problem and soon found the answer.'

For the dual purpose of stimulating controversy and promoting the fortunes of his *Outline of History*, expensively sponsored by Newnes, H. G. Wells named his six great men. They were Jesus of Nazareth, Gautama Buddha, Aristotle, Asoka, Roger Bacon, Abraham Lincoln. On his own upward way, Winston Churchill paused to write *My Escape from the Boers*, announced in the magazine as 'the full story now told for the first time'. Conan Doyle followed with the serialisation of his autobiography, *Memories and Adventures*, in which there occurred the declaration: 'Wonderful is the atmosphere of war. When the millennium comes the world will gain much, but it will lose its greatest thrill.'

He had resolved to bring the curtain down at last on Sherlock Holmes, the most absurdly memorable fiction character of our time. Accepting the inevitable, Greenhough Smith persuaded him to choose what he considered the twelve best Holmes stories, sealing the list in an envelope, and confiding it to a locked drawer in the editor's room. Readers were then invited to send in their lists, a prize of £100 being offered for the one that most nearly coincided with the author's.

Lists came in from far and near. The winner was R. T. Norman, of Spring Hill, Wellingborough, Northants, who correctly named in order ten out of Conan Doyle's twelve, which gave first place to *The Speckled Band* and the last place to *The Reigate Squires*. Scores of readers placed eight correctly. All included *The Speckled Band*, *The Red-Headed League*, *The Final Problem*, *A Scandal in Bohemia*, and *The Five Orange Pips*.

The last of the fifty-six Sherlock Holmes stories published in *The Strand* through thirty-six years appeared in the issue for April 1927. It was entitled *The Adventure of Shoscombe Old Place* (£628 14s for the British and Colonial serial rights; 5s a word for the American rights). The illustrator was F. Wiles, whose line was less gaunt than Sidney Paget's, his Holmes being slightly more refined in features.

'Sherlock Holmes had been bending for a long time over a low-powered microscope. Now he straightened himself up and looked round in triumph. "It's glue, Watson," said he. "Unquestionably it is glue." ' Seven thousand words later, Conan

Doyle wrote: ' . . . So the lucky owner got away scatheless from this strange incident in a career which has now outlived its shadows and ended in an honoured old age'. *The Strand* published the author's valedictory:

'Sherlock Holmes began his adventures in the very heart of the later Victorian Era, carried them all through the all-too-short reign of Edward, and has managed to hold his own little niche even in these feverish days. Thus it would be true to say that those who first read of him as a young man have lived to see their grown-up children following the same adventures in the same magazine. It is a sterling example of the patience and loyalty of the British public.'

A similar tribute could have been paid to Doyle. Despite many inducements, he had remained faithful to *The Strand* from the beginning of his association with it back in 1891. And, having abandoned Holmes, he continued to write other stories for the magazine up to the year of his death.

3

Spectacular accessions to the fiction department were announced, not necessarily as compensation for the disappearance of Sherlock Holmes, whose magnetism had certainly lost some of its force. A lack of story-telling stature was strongly hinted at in the *London Mercury*: 'W. J. Locke and A. E. W. Mason seem like the last of the mammoths.' Among the new writers one was aware of premeditated artifice, of great technical skill, often delightful idiosyncrasy, but of less virility and warmth, less heart.

Michael Arlen was one of the newly emblazoned names, the exotic young author of *The Green Hat* who joked with equal readiness about his Armenian birth and his subservience to the code of the English gentleman. (There were kinds of behaviour about which he could be smartingly strict.) For a hectic Mayfly span he soared high in the social and literary firmament. His short stories, no matter how short, sold for £900 apiece (world rights), whether or not they were published. He rode about the West End in a primrose yellow Rolls-Royce. He knew all the head waiters and scorned the *parvenu* habit of shaking hands with them. He received gallery plaudits at theatre first nights. His manners were beyond reproach. He wore the best shirts and ties that Bond Street could offer. His conversation was witty. His smile invited friendship, which he was likely to encourage by transferring the carnation from his lapel to yours.

I met him at luncheon parties given by Lady Lavery, the once beautiful wife, then still glamorous, of Sir John Lavery, R.A., at 5 Cromwell Place, South Kensington. He glowed with success, not egotistically. When, overnight, he was bereft of it, his self-command remained unimpaired. His book sales had begun to sag, but he was still in the market. He then wrote a novel that was bought for newspaper serialisation. It failed badly with the readers and was cut short in mid-course; a direful setback for a young novelist. He did not complain, did not rail against the gods, did not appear to be perplexed by their capriciousness. No doubt he was buttressed by ancestral fatalism. He carried himself well and did not write another novel.

Aldous Huxley was in the literary swim, and by then quite a sizeable fish, having written *Limbo*, *Mortal Coils*, *Antic Hay*, *Crome Yellow*, and *These Barren Leaves*. His name in *The Strand* was a sign that the *coterie* minds were adapting their techniques to a wider market without losing caste. In fact, the highbrow short story writers had become as formula-ridden as their commercial counterparts, whom they disdained. Not that Huxley aspired to popularity in the magazine sense. For him the crowd, the human mass, was repellent. He aspired to the cheques it guaranteed. When they did not arrive promptly, he would write petulant little reminders from his club, the Athenaeum.

Towards the unexpected end of his life, I spent an evening listening to his talk at the home of friends of mine, Dr and Mrs William Sargant, in Hamilton Terrace, N.W. He was interested in Will Sargant's book, *The Battle for the Mind*, the publication of which I had recommended to Heinemann, under whose imprint it appeared. Huxley's talk over the dinner table flowed as from a crystal spring. His precision of speech, donnish to some ears, confirmed the vintage quality of his thought and the delicacy of his understanding. His voice was a finely tuned instrument, fascinating to hear. And he was humorous. He rose up to illustrate by stance and gesture a reminiscence of Arnold Bennett, a perfect little vignette of mimicry. Recalling it, I now smile with wan regret, where then I laughed. Afterwards, I looked up references to him in Bennett's journals, e.g.: 'Aldous Huxley is getting more and more into the habit of using such words as "inconceivable", "incredible", "fantastic". These are his favourite words, and one of them comes into nearly every sentence. His general knowledge is extraordinarily good. In fact it is inconceivable, incredible and fantastic.' (1927.)

Huxley had purged his speech of those adjectives, while agreeing, nodding emphatically, that life becomes more mysterious as one gets older; indeed, that it is more inconceivable, more incredible, more fantastic. The display of his mind through four and a half hours was something to remember. As we parted, driving home past midnight, I almost dreaded the slump into banality that would follow. Hardly anyone seemed worth listening to for days after.

4

There were quaint propinquities in *The Strand* of the late '20s: W. H. Hudson, pronouncing upon intelligence in cats, and P. G. Wodehouse reiterating the lack of it in his 'old beans' and 'old fruits'; J. J. Bell, more sophisticated than devotees of his 'Wee Macgreegor' stories may have supposed, and Hugh Walpole, as eager to be liked as to succeed; A. B. Walkley, dramatic critic of *The Times*, bringing his Olympian authority to bear on the subject of stage kissing, and E. Phillips Oppenheim, spurning the notion that he took his characters from life—'what a lot of puppets they would be!'

Oppenheim contributed copiously to *The Strand* between the wars. His family background was Faringdon, in Berkshire, with City connections in the leather trade, at which 'Oppy' (to his friends) worked until he was 35. He then wrote a novel which was taken as a serial for the *Sheffield Weekly Telegraph*, price £250. To him it seemed easy money. He wrote more serials at the same price.

Applying business methods to literature, he settled down to write two novels a year by dictating an average of 4,000 words a day, four days a week. He kept it up for thirty years, during most of which he lived in style on the Riviera. He never sketched a plot. He decided on two or three characters and set them working out their own fortunes according to the formula:

> Our deeds still follow from afar,
> What we have been makes us what we are.

Apparently as a demonstration of that philosophy, he wrote a novel, *The Lost Leader*, in which A. J. Balfour was the model for the chief character. Oppenheim became a brand-name for a dependable two-dimensional kind of fiction that rarely stood up to the tests of logic, consistency, plausibility. It was produced with business-like regularity and a sharp eye on the market. The big public that he gathered round him by his prolific inventiveness and steady application did not remember the title of his last book while eagerly anticipating the next.

The juxtaposition of Herbert Shaw and A. M. Burrage was apt enough, two Bohemian temperaments that suffused and at times confused gifts from which more was expected than came forth. They had a precise knowledge of the popular short story as the product of calculated design. Both privately despised it, though it was their living. Shaw, half Irish and often quoting Swinburne with excitement in his voice and tears in his eyes, wrote comparatively little, beset by the fear that his best would never be good enough.

Burrage, a phlegmatic Englishman, could write the romantic stuff in his sleep; and, oddly, he paraded the world in what often seemed like semi-somnambulism. He wrote, anonymously, a well-received First World War autobiography. He is remembered now mainly by a witticism preserved in a dwindling club circle. Confronted by an overdue bill at the Savage, he asked for a cheque form. He was slow in filling it in at the cashier's desk. Sounds of impatience came from members behind him. 'Sorry,' Burrage said over his shoulder, 'I'm trying to think of a likely bank.'

One of the youngest fiction writers to crash *The Strand*

barrier (never an easy thing to do) was Marten Cumberland, an apprentice from the sea, where he read avidly in the long watches as a radio operator. He had the fecundity and inventiveness of Simenon. Paris supplied him with the material for his long, apparently inexhaustible, series of novels written round the character of Commissaire Saturnin Drax. The quotations at the head of his chapters are more than the pickings of his wide reading. They speak of a poetic sensibility which one wishes he had other opportunities of indulging.

Fiction in *The Strand* seldom touched the deeper currents of life and thought. That function was allotted to the article writers and those industrious symposium arrangers. Blood sports, for instance; that recurring theme of British domestic controversy. Dean Inge, of St Paul's, Sir William Orpen, R.A., Conan Doyle, and Sir George Greenwood, of the Royal Society for the Prevention of Cruelty to Animals, urged abolition. Stalwarts of the other side of the argument were the diehard novelist, Horace Annesley Vachell, Sir Claude Champion De Crespigny, 'A Spanish Diplomat', defending bull-fighting, and 'A Master of Foxhounds', whose anonymity hardly helped the case.

As any newspaper editor would have forecast from experience, the response was prompt and vigorous and a cause of angry recrimination when readers found that no space was to be given to their views. Shrinking from the uproar, and giving a never-again decision, Greenhough Smith tossed a less disturbing pebble into the pond, asking a number of authors, among them, inexplicably, only one woman, the question: Which character in all fiction would you most like to have created?

The novelty has by no means faded from their replies. Conan Doyle—Colonel Newcome; H. G. Wells—Falstaff; Arnold Bennett—Alyosha from *The Brothers Karamazov*; John Masefield—Homer's Achilles; H. de Vere Stacpoole—D'Artagnan; W. B. Maxwell—John Inglesant; E. F. Benson—Charles, 'the true heir', from *Ravenshoe*; E. Temple Thurston—Sir Willoughby Patterne; Hugh Walpole—Don Quixote; Marjorie Bowen—Lovelace from *Clarissa Harlowe*; E. Phillips Oppenheim—Sherlock Holmes; W. J. Locke—D'Artagnan;

Edgar Wallace—'any of Dickens's characters'; John Buchan— Jeanie Deans; Denis Mackail—Catriona; Cosmo Hamilton— Becky Sharp.

A more resounding splash was made with *Modern Art, For and Against*, in which P. G. Konody, art critic of *The Observer* and the *Daily Mail*, was challenged with the contention that 'a form of art has arisen which, consisting as it so largely does, of gross distortions and geometrical puzzles, is likely to be subversive of the mental and even the physical welfare of the country'. Examples of the work of Paul Klee, André Masson, Suzanne Roger, and Lawrence Atkinson—'apostles of non-representational art'—were used as illustrations.

The art critic's rejoinder was judicially unprovocative. 'Appreciation of art, after all, is merely a matter of getting used to it.' He cited with effect the famous onslaught on *Christ in the Carpenter's Shop*, by Millais. 'It touches the lowest depths of what is mean, odious, repulsive and revolting. This, in the 19th century, and in the 82nd year of the Royal Academy of Art, is the most that the pre-Raphaelites can do to render reverence and homage to the faith in which we live and die!' (Charles Dickens) 'Getting used' to the Pre-Raphaelites was in the same frame of reference as the derision that greeted Wagner's music when it was first heard in London, and the proposition that 'it is not the pictures but the artists who should be hung'.

Rising above the unworthy polemics, Konody, who combined art criticism with the no less venturesome business of advising rich men on their picture purchases, submitted it as his opinion that 'the range of the artist's activity as regards self-expression has no necessary limits, that anything is material for the artist's vision, that everything is grist to his mill, that the only aspect of his work that matters is the communication between his spirit and the spirit of the spectator'.

Sincerity was a Victorian characteristic that prevailed in most areas of public self-expression when *The Strand* was founded. Now there seemed to be a danger of its being overcome by plausibility. Whether or not as intuitive editorial protest, the magazine abandoned the unending art debate, assured of a more appreciative audience for 'the first illustrated article on the inner workings of the B.B.C.', and for its inquiry into the best-selling gramophone records of 1929. Topping the list were *Hear My Prayer*, sung by the choir of the Temple Church, London, and *Valencia*, 'the most popular record ever made by H.M.V.' up to that time.

Time's perspectives are jolted by the reminder that Croydon aerodrome then merited the description of 'the world's greatest airport'. In 1929, readers of *The Strand* were taken 'behind the scenes' there in an article that made the point that 'aviation today is a great paradox. It represents the biggest and most spectacular human advance ever made—and yet, although it has become so commonplace that the drone of an aero-engine now excites in most of us little or no more interest than that of a motorcar, look at the extremely small number of people who have as yet flown!' Today, not yet forty years later, Croydon aerodrome has virtually gone back to grass, its erasure almost as complete as if it had been decreed by nature and not by man.

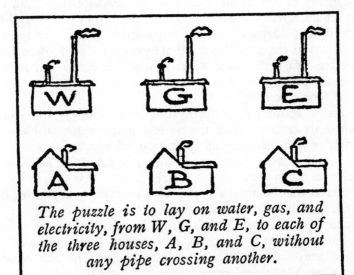

The puzzle is to lay on water, gas, and electricity, from W, G, and E, to each of the three houses, A, B, and C, without any pipe crossing another.

A puzzle devised by Henry Dudeney, the 'Puzzle King' of *The Strand Magazine*, for 'Perplexities', a regular feature for many years.

FIFTEEN

Churchill as a Contributor

I

The famous cover was redesigned more than once to give full scope to four-colour printing. A double-decker bus replaced the hansom cab of the old cover. The two church towers were retained, emblems of historical continuity. In the foreground, instead of the running newsboy, was an elegant girl who might have been tripping along to a rehearsal at the Vaudeville Theatre. Bulldog Drummond, revolver in hand, appeared on the cover of one issue, a daring break with vaunted tradition. Another redrawing of the cover brought the lofty Law Courts clock into nearer perspective. Equally bold interior decoration with colour and photogravure gave the magazine a newly furnished look. That the price was raised at last to a shilling seemed both logical and fair.

Change had come to the famous street from which the magazine took its name forty years before. The two churches were marooned in the traffic tide. Romano's, just round the corner from Southampton Street, was little more than a name with a brazen past. Rule's, two hundred yards away in Maiden Lane, had a crudely unsympathetic new proprietor, since deceased, who was alienating the Bohemian spirit long implanted there. Across the Strand, what was once London's most popular music-hall, the Tivoli, had become a cinema. Kipling's fifth-floor chambers in Villiers Street were occupied by a clergyman who had to endure the nuisance of strangers knocking at his door.

Opposite *The Strand* office were the premises of Weldon's Pattern Shop, with the long wall mirrors still in place where Edwardian ladies studied their forms and figures as part of the service. In the vaults of Coutts's Bank were souvenirs of an earlier age deposited there by customers more than two centuries ago and not inspected since. Epstein's bitterly debated statuary on the British Medical Association building was beginning to yield to the ruthless criticism of atmospheric pollution.

The Strand was still one of central London's greatest if unloveliest arterial ways. For all its thousand years of daily use, it had never pretended to lead any man's feet to the New Jerusalem. Its pavements were thronged, its sounds raucous, its air stale with old petrol fumes, its shop-window displays mostly second-rate, its westward view of the sky beyond Nelson's silhouette often breath-taking at the sunset hour. Not its chromium-plate, its garish new façades, or its neon lights, finally dispelled the raffishness that had clung to it from its back alley past, when it was the tradesmen's entrance to the great houses of the seventeenth-centu˞ Thames-side grandees.

2

In the 1930s, the popular newspapers, enlarged to twenty, twenty-four and sometimes to twenty-eight pages, were taking over the magazine function. Their leader pages were transformed into arenas of the liveliest controversy, in which the participants were often important public figures. In other pages there were serial stories by distinguished authors, short stories, and a miscellany of 'feature' stuff that formerly belonged to the magazine domain. The *Daily Express*, striving towards its second million, led a development that, in conjunction with such other manifestations of the spirit of the age as the motoring revolution, broadcasting, the imminence of television, and paperback books, would finally sound the knell of the popular monthly magazine.

The first seismic warnings of shaken foundations· came through the advertising department. *The Strand* was no longer turning away space buyers. In some issues it could fill no more than thirty or forty pages with advertising, a vast difference from the old lush days. There was also a qualitative change; more proprietary medicines and hygienic and surgical appliances. More was made of sponsored advertising: Derek Oldham, of the Savoy Opera, extolling the virtues of Ovaltine, and Compton Mackenzie pointing the way to self-improvement through Pelmanism. There was an increase in the number of advertisements for educational and vocational training courses, which did not command the maximum space rates.

The big spenders on advertising, the car manufacturers, the oil companies, the food industry, the department stores, were being persuaded that, although *The Strand* was read by more persons per copy than a newspaper and had a longer life, the monthly interval was no longer economically tenable. A faster beat was heard not only in the dance halls but in the factories, in the laboratories, in the colleges and schools, in the office and in the home. *The Strand* belonged to a more leisurely age. How long could it survive the quickened pace of existence? The question was more than a rhetorical one in the '30s.

3

Conan Doyle died in 1930; for *The Strand Magazine* the end of a long and exemplary relationship between author and editor. He was commemorated by a full-page photograph in which he looked like a universal uncle, and by the reprinting of *A Scandal in Bohemia*, the first Sherlock Holmes story that appeared in *The Strand*. It was illustrated by the original Paget drawings.

That year Greenhough Smith retired from active editorial work, retaining his Newnes directorship and continuing to advise on policy. The task of producing the magazine was assigned to Reeves Shaw, a Newnes executive of long experience whose energy was spread over a number of other publications, including *The Humourist* and *London Opinion*. Shaw did not have Greenhough Smith's dignified authority or his statesmanlike attitude to his job, seeing it as a public responsibility as well as part of a commercial enterprise. But neither was Shaw one of the new technicians of print and layout masquerading as editors, while in truth being puppets of a proprietor or a board.

Unbowed by his eighty years, Greenhough Smith died in 1935. The obituarists could find only conventional phrases for his epitaph. 'A distinguished and memorable figure . . . beloved by those who knew him intimately . . . respected by all.' His professional life had been enviably free from crises. His last years were clouded by the loneliness of one who outlives his friends.

Reeves Shaw summoned a variety of talents to help in the production of the magazine. On the art side, there was George Leech, an accomplished painter who had a sound knowledge of process work and a following among the newer generation of illustrators. One of the new editorial men was George Blake, the Scots novelist who wrote *The Shipbuilders*, another, Hugh Ross Williamson, who has since made a reputation as dramatist and popular historian. Shaw himself had a shrewd eye for the best-seller qualities in fiction. He objected to married heroes in short stories. Characters had to be recognisable types, settings familiar but not drab. A keen judge of topical humour, he bought the work of D. B. Wyndham Lewis, K. R. G. Browne (a grandson of 'Phiz', the Dickens illustrator), Maurice Lane-Norcott, and Anthony Armstrong.

It was his practised editorial judgment that brought Winston Churchill back into *The Strand* at a time when that politician's prestige was low in the land, the period in which Churchill himself announced: 'I am finished.' Shaw gave the magazine a sense of urgency that it had never had and that befitted the times. Communications were swifter and more complex. World events were being reported with an immediacy that was new in human experience. Those were matters of more than objective editorial interest. They involved factors of serious import for the magazine future.

The son of a Brighton bookseller, Shaw lived a life of exuberant generosity that occasionally contracted into alarming enmities. He was splendid at helping lame dogs over stiles, and there were artists and writers who had cause to remember him gratefully. Friendship was another thing. It was liable to be struck down by a sudden flash of bitterness coming out of a clear sky.

For example, he was at supper at the Café Royal with a

The traffic problem in the 1930s : Heath Robinson suggests a solution.
—*Reproduced by permission of Mrs W. Heath Robinson.*

Two fiction characters popular with readers of *The Strand:* (above) P. G. Wodehouse's 'Jeeves', and (below) 'Sapper's' ex-officer vigilante, 'Bulldog Drummond'.

companion from Fleet Street who was affably greeted by
C. R. W. Nevinson, the once famous 'rebel' painter. Suddenly
incensed, Shaw seized the water carafe to throw it at
Nevinson, his eyes blazing hate of what he called 'these bloody
celebrities'. He seemed to be in the grip of a deep disgust at
his own comparative anonymity. 'I would have given five
hundred pounds to put my name to that book of yours,' he
told the author of a well-reviewed, inconsiderable novel.

The incident at the Café Royal led to an estrangement
between Shaw and his friend that lasted two years. At the
end of that time Shaw telephoned to propose a reunion. It
took place in a wine bar at the foot of Ludgate Hill. Shaw
insisted on ordering a succession of half-bottles of champagne.
His friend begged to be allowed to buy the sixth and last.
Amity having been restored, Shaw warmly agreed. They drank
it, their quarrel was revived, and they did not speak for a
further six months.

4

Shaw not only commissioned the Churchill articles (at
from £250 to £400 apiece, depending on the length) but often
supplied the subjects. Sometimes they were discussed at
Churchill's flat in Morpeth Mansions, Westminster. I remember Shaw telling me, in no mood of complaint: 'He expected
me to drink half a tumbler of port with him at eleven in the
morning.' Churchill wrote on past and contemporary statesmen, on the world as he expected it to be in the 1980s, on
the American spirit, on the men who influenced him. His
articles were sometimes printed in the bold type that they
merited as substantial expressions of his far-ranging views.
Already he was projecting his thoughts towards the hydrogen
bomb.

'What is lacking is the method to set the bonfire alight, or
it may be the detonator to cause the dynamite to explode.
The scientists are looking for this.' He foresaw the coming
feasibility of 'schemes of cosmic magnitude'. Geography and
climate would obey man's orders. 'Fifty thousand tons of
water, the amount displaced by the Berengaria, would, if

exploited as described, suffice to shift Ireland into the middle of the Atlantic.' The reference to Ireland in that context may or may not have been psychologically illuminating. There was the peroration: 'Without an equal growth of Mercy, Pity, Peace and Love, science itself may destroy all that makes human life majestic and tolerable.'

He movingly recollected, in another article, his last talks with Balfour. 'I saw with grief the approaching departure, and, for all human purposes, extinction of a being far uplifted above the common run. As I observed him regarding with calm, firm, and cheerful gaze the approach of Death, I felt— and it is a fortifying thought—how foolish the Stoics were to make so much fuss about an event so natural and so indispensable to mankind.' John Buchan told me, some time before Churchill's article appeared, that as he lay dying Balfour sent for Stanley Baldwin, to whom he said: 'I am looking forward with the greatest interest and curiosity to the experience that lies in front of me.'

Reeves Shaw asked Churchill to write an article on what he would do were he able to start life again. He accepted the invitation with great good humour. One of his personal habits that he reviewed was smoking. 'I suppose I ought to give it up. Look at all the money I have wasted on tobacco. Think of it all invested and mounting up at compound interest year after year.' He recalled his father, 'his eyes gleaming through the haze of his cigarette', saying: 'Why begin? If you want to have an eye that is true, and a hand that does not quiver, don't smoke.' Lord Roberts had stopped him in St James's Street with the admonition: 'Don't smoke. I'm sure your father injured his health by oversmoking. Give it up now and live long in full vigour and activity.'

He wrote in his article of the soothing influence of tobacco on his nervous system. He believed that it kept him in good temper. He also believed that the smoking habit saved his life in Flanders, that if he had not turned back to retrieve a box of matches from a dugout he would have walked into the shell that exploded a hundred yards away. As for living his life again, 'the journey has been enjoyable and well worth making—once!'

Surveying the American scene, he decided that its people were 'a frailer race with a lighter structure' than our own. The English people were tough, reserved and dogged, 'with many latent resources'. While it seemed to him likely and even certain that 'the first prizes of the future' would go to the United States, he declared his belief that 'Englishmen will still remain a vast enduring force for virility and sanity and goodwill' among the nations.

He recalled in another article an American politician of the '90s, Bourke Cockran, as one of the men who had influenced him. They met when Churchill first went to America in 1895. A gifted and impressive man, Bourke Cockran changed his political colours more than once, swinging from the Democrats to the Republicans and back again.

Churchill wrote as if he had been inspired by the character and courage shown by Bourke Cockran in taking steps that might have been fatal to his prospects. A decade later Churchill reproduced a similar pattern of shifting allegiance in his own political life. The other men he named as his activating exemplars were Sir Francis Mowatt, 'a Treasury official of the old school', sometime Gladstone's private secretary; Lord Hugh Cecil, 'a real Tory'; and Lloyd George.

Relaxing from sterner affairs, he scrutinised the work and motives of the cartoonists, whose attentions for the time being were not being pressed upon him. He measured the forlorn figure of Strube's 'Little Man' (*Daily Express*) against that of the traditional John Bull, 'with his big stick and resolute, rugged face'. He thought Low (*Evening Standard*) brilliant and mischievous, 'a little postwar Australian radical', and revealed that his great friend Lord Birkenhead deeply resented Low's cartoons of him. 'Certainly the loathing and contempt which our transplanted Australian put into his pencil were obvious; and when the cartoons extended to deriding the entire Smith family without respect of age or sex, he had good reason for complaint. He never forgave the insults.'

Agreeing that there was 'enough truth in some cartoons to be more funny to others than to oneself', he dismissed the cartooning tribe as 'grave and gay, kind and spiteful, true and misleading'. It was a light amusing essay adequate to its theme. His cheerful readiness to be made fun of by others left one wondering: Did he ever laugh at himself?

When he delivered, by request, four thousand words on *The Truth About Hitler* (£250), it was thought advisable to announce, on publication, that his views were not necessarily endorsed by the magazine, an indication of the dangerous excitability of the new regime in Germany. He referred to Hitler as 'a child of the rage and grief' of a people humiliated by defeat in war. 'He it was who exorcised the spirit of despair from the German mind by substituting the not less hateful but far less morbid spirit of revenge.'

That he was enabled to do so, he pointed out, was due to 'the lethargy and folly' of the French and British Governments; and Churchill could not conceal his impatience with the 'absurd delusion' of the French that vast monetary compensation could still be extracted from the Germans for the evil they had wrought. The terrible 'blood bath' of the Nazis on the night of June 30, 1934, was evidence for him of infamous tyranny, for which there could be no excuse in the court of civilised opinion.

Would Hitler involve the world in another great war? 'It is on this mystery of the future,' Churchill wrote, 'that history will pronounce him either a monster or a hero.'

Churchill incurred editorial displeasure by sending a copy of his Hitler article to America, where it was published before its appearance in *The Strand*, which had contractually acquired the first use. On receiving the editor's pained reminder, he offered to forgo part of his payment from *The Strand*. 'He would have been surprised and displeased had we accepted the offer,' was a comment made in the office at the time. As it happened, the leading American magazines rejected the article. It was published in a comparatively obscure journal. 'He could be annoying in ways like that,' I was told by an old member of the staff. There were no such complications in my dealings with him.

Re-reading that article, I recalled his deliberately nasal enunciation of 'Nazi', as if it were distasteful to him to speak the name. In 1933, I had regular talks on the telephone with him about the articles he was contributing to the *Daily Mail*. Writing this, I hear again the scornful inflexion of his voice coming over the line from Chartwell: 'Those dirty little Narzis'.

The Truth About Hitler incited a protest from the German embassy in London and the banning of *The Strand* in the Fatherland. Whether or not as a placatory gesture to the Foreign Office (rather than the Wilhelmstrasse), *The Strand* followed Churchill's article with one entitled *Hitler's Man of Strength*, namely, Ribbentrop. It was replete with photographs of him in various poses, including that of the devoted family man.

The writer of the article was a soft-voiced, auburn-bearded, respected journalist named George Slocombe, who had the credentials of the *Manchester Guardian* and other responsible newpapers behind him. He was sufficiently impressed by Hitler's ambassador in London to write of him: 'He is still young—at forty-four—still unembittered, still undisillusioned, ambitious and adventurous-minded; handsomely endowed both mentally and physically, both socially and financially. He represents modern Germany to the world in its most attractive light.' Read today, the article has the hollow ring of a diplomatic compliment.

More engaging to read, more rewarding, was the article in which Churchill disported himself under the heading, *The Truth About Myself*, obviously an inspiration from *The Strand* office. He let it be known that the major disappointment of his career up to that time was the failure at the Dardanelles, 'a horrible experience to undergo'. He had seen 'the truth, shining clear and bright', in contrast with the terrible slaughter and desolation elsewhere. 'And here was the way out, the path to victory—and even more than victory—to early peace.' Speaking of the doleful sequel, he wrote that 'they clobbered it all to the ground and their children and their children's children will long rue the day!'

He declaimed against the misleading notion (revived in the years to come) that he took pleasure in war, stating categorically: 'I do not delight in war.' He ardently desired its abolition from the affairs of nations and the lives of men.

And in a grinning aside he disowned another public fiction concerning himself: 'I do not delight in hats.'

5

Three men of the period who were readily warrantable subjects for articles were Franklin Delano Roosevelt, Neville Chamberlain, and J. P. Kennedy, the then new American ambassador in London. Roosevelt was presented as 'the easiest of all American presidents for the Englishman to understand', a supposition based on the argument that he was at heart a squire with broad acres on the banks of the Hudson River. It was further sustained by references to timber plantations and Jersey and Holstein pedigree herds.

Chamberlain was credited with a sense of humour that was 'dry but eminently respectable'. His character was defined as 'sincere and unsubtle'. He had no vices to provide the material of compulsive reading.

The word sketch of Kennedy, the ambassador, was equally ineffectual in projecting him as a candidate for British acclaim. 'This original, successful American business man, bringing to new and wider problems the skill which has helped to solve old problems is, one feels, fundamentally deep-rooted, and, thus entrenched, is able to look forward with serenity and hope.' History was to reserve for another member of his family the attributes that make a man memorable.

Churchill on Eden reads today like an exercise in loyalty rather than in heartfelt admiration, for all the unstinted praise it expressed and its warm commendation of its subject's public virtue. At that time the future Lord Avon was the most publicised British politician. He was having what Churchill described as 'an astonishing vogue' in the United States. Churchill saw him as 'the only representative of the mutilated generation who has achieved a first-class political position'.

It was an opportunity for Churchill to express himself in elegiac terms about the nation's losses in the First World War. 'The scythe of the Great War shore away the flower of a whole generation of British youth', depriving the country of 'men of force and ability who would now be reaching their prime'. The era of Baldwin and MacDonald had been 'singularly barren' of new men. There was a decline of spirit and debating power in the House of Commons.

He wrote in the magazine about the great new liner *Queen Mary*—'the symbol of our renaissance', a sign that England had at last recovered from her postwar lassitude. He greeted with warm respect the new monarch, King George VI, whose accession had overridden his devoted championship of Edward VIII. His article on *Women in War* mingled sublime sentiment with parenthetical jollity:

As sweet Polly Oliver lay musing in bed,
A strange passing fancy came into her head:
Nor father nor mother shall make me false prove!
I'll enlist for a soldier and follow my love.

The articles were dictated; he said so in one of them. They gave him 'speaking practice'. His only use for a pen was to correct and interpolate. One was constantly aware of his voice. Adjectives were flying buttresses of the argument. Without them his vocabulary would have been fairly commonplace.

Compared with Churchill, Lloyd George did not exist as a journalist, though he liked to write articles and still more liked to be told that what he wrote was good. I telephoned him one Sunday afternoon at Churt from the *Daily Mail* office. He answered the call personally in a disguised voice. 'I'll see if he's in.' 'I'm quite sure he's in, Mr Lloyd George,' I said and laughed. There was a moment's silence; then he laughed too. I wrote in my diary: 'I told him we were glad to have his article, that it was just right, etc. He seemed to like appreciation, so I gave him a good dose.'

One of his *Strand* articles, *Why War?* showed him groping like the rest of us in the psychotic atmosphere of the late 1930s. 'Wherever one goes and almost whomever one meets, war is discussed. Worse still, it is, like death, taken for granted. Is there any issue between arming nations which cannot be settled by peaceable methods?' Despite the current alarms, he believed that there would be peace 'for another decade'. As his recently published *War Memoirs* had shown, the music in his voice was not imparted to his prose.

6

From about 1935, the editorial emphasis was on fiction. Proportionately fewer articles were being commissioned. Kipling's last short story for *The Strand*, called *Teem—A Treasure Hunter*, appeared in the month of his death, breaking another important link with the magazine's early days. P. G. Wodehouse was writing as freshly as ever, after over thirty years as a contributor; an extraordinary record. Other familiar story names that had retained their hold were A. E. W. Mason, W. J. Locke, J. J. Bell, John Buchan, Gilbert Frankau, Michael Arlen.

John Buchan (later Lord Tweedsmuir) led a dual life as romantic author and practical publisher (Thomas Nelson & Sons, Ltd.). Over three or four years I met him often, and always with intellectual profit to myself. He was first-rate in conversation, drawing on rich layers of personal experience. He was more ready to discuss Imperial politics than, for instance, his work as a novelist. He was not much given to talking about himself, though there was a period of what seemed to be semi-hypochondria, when his health was a fairly constant topic. He had known many of the leading men of his time and liked to gossip about them, without stooping to the scandal level. In his earliest London years he was a manuscript reader for John Lane.

He had kept from his Milner days in South Africa an ardour for the public service. To me he seemed to be a careerist with an uncommon lack of self-interest. One felt that he was marked out for spectacular advancement, though it certainly was not clear then that destiny had him in view for the splendours of a governor-generalship. He had the dignity and integrity, everything but the build.

In describing himself to me as a Tory Democrat he seemed to consider it a precise definition. Some thought it a kind of sophistry. His romantic heart, like Conan Doyle's, reacted impatiently from the more inglorious aspects of democracy. 'The horrors of war are obvious enough,' he had written, 'but it may reasonably be argued that they are not greater than the horrors of peace.' He was not yet the historian of the

1914–18 war, in which role he excelled Conan Doyle. Behind the heady sentiment was the belief that mankind's greatest problem is intellectual inequality and that there is a need for an autocratic élite to assist in resolving it.

As an adventure writer Buchan composed his stories in a prose that was superior to much in the *genre*. With it went an imagination that was harnessed by his tidy, well-organised habits of thought. The short story was not his ideal medium but he never wrote a dull one. He knew the secret. He was a born story-teller. 'The season was absurdly early, for the blackthorn was in flower and the hedgerows were full of primroses. The partridges were paired, the rooks were well on with their nests. . . .' Pushing aside the greenwood boughs, we follow Richard Hannay under a spell that we know will tighten its hold with every step we take.

7

In *The Strand* fiction firmament a glittering new galaxy appeared in those uncertain years. Warwick Deeping, Rafael Sabatini, Agatha Christie, Leslie Charteris, Margery Allingham, A. G. Macdonell, Margery Sharp, Carter Dickson, Storm Jameson, Dale Collins, Dorothy Sayers, F. Brett Young, Margaret Kennedy, Alec Waugh, Dorothy Black, C. S. Forester: the short story content of the magazine was never more richly varied.

In that brave contemporary array the name of Leonard Merrick suddenly appears like a vagary of natural selection. He was writing before 1914, acquiring a reputation as 'the novelists' novelist' (fastened on him by Barrie) and having no real public success in consequence. One remembered *Conrad In Search Of His Youth*, long since dated, and the little volume of his delightful, but also faded, Parisian short stories, *A Call from the Past*. To me, his was the least clear identity among the writers of the period. I never met anyone who could speak intimately of him, though he was admired by his fellow writers and was paid the very rare compliment of a collected edition in his lifetime.

Warwick Deeping haunts the farther recesses of my

memory like a phantom. In my early boyhood at Vinehall Farm, near Robertsbridge, Sussex, where I was born, I often saw him walking between the hedges of the Hastings road, a silent figure in an old raincoat who stared straight ahead through gold-rimmed *pince-nez* like one for whom journey's end was beyond the known horizons. Locally, he was recognised as a non-practising doctor rather than as an unsuccessful novelist. Maurice Hewlett was the pattern figure in his professional life. Fortune came at long last with *Sorrel & Son*, a postwar novel that sounded chords of sentiment matching the mood of national convalescence. It was the crux of an otherwise inadequately rewarded career and presumably endowed him comfortably through the years that remained.

For Rafael Sabatini's picturesque talent that was an inhibiting time. He was extremely sensitive to its tensions and felt the menace of the future more keenly than most of us. He could find no refuge from it in his work as historical novelist. His was an attractive personality, made the more so by his fine perceptive intelligence. The swashbuckling characters in his stories were not projections of a wish for personal aggrandisement. He was a man of the study and the library. He found his sword-play in conversation, a declining social amenity that kept him increasingly away from London, to the regret of us who knew him. 'Raffles' Sabatini's friendship had the quality of a privilege. He was a dear, delightful man.

SIXTEEN

Jubilee Year Brings Change

I

From the threshold of its fiftieth year of publication—a record easily eclipsed by *The Cornhill* and *Blackwood's*, for example, and by *Harper's* and *Scribner's* in America—*The Strand* looked back in no spirit of jubilation in the Christmas issue for 1940. 'The magazine has had to celebrate both its Silver Jubilee (1915) and its Jubilee in years when the country is at death grips with Germany. May it soon welcome a return to peaceful days with a Victory Number, and then proceed to its Diamond Jubilee and eventually its Centenary in those happier times of which Mr Winston Churchill speaks in his congratulatory message.' The Second World War was imposing restrictions that discouraged optimism if they did not diminish the pride demonstrated in the boldly displayed tribute from its most famous contributor, who by then was Prime Minister.

Old readers may have found it congenial to be reminded of a time when England's wars were no more than punitive expeditions, when income tax was sixpence in the pound, and Lord Randolph Churchill was being eulogised as 'the leader of men in a very special sense'. Some looked back to 1891 as a year of scarlet and gold pageantry, in which the German Emperor, on a State visit, was the plumed and prancing central figure. Others recalled it also as the year in which the old Queen launched the world's most formidable battleship, the *Royal Sovereign*.

It was an occasion for recollecting the royal favour shown to *The Strand* through its five decades. As Prince of Wales, the Duke of Windsor had allowed the diary kept by him during his African travels to form the basis of several articles, illustrated by his own photographs. More recently still, an article was published 'with the sanction of Their Royal Highnesses, the Duke and Duchess of York', then living at 145 Piccadilly, where the Duke received the message that led to his accession to the Throne. The article described the upbringing of their two daughters. 'And so they stand there together in the small secluded garden of their London home, two little English children, two small sisters, hand in hand, facing the coming years.'

For all its accustomed unction, the old manner had not been quite so sentimental. *The Strand* was relaxing its long prevailing masculine bias. If there were new readers to be found they would most probably be women, whose interests were dominating an increasingly large section of the periodical publishing industry.

That Christmas issue, with its 160 pages of reading matter and 40 pages of advertising, was in the old 'double number' tradition and comparatively sumptuous beside the 72-page issues that increased paper costs had imposed during the first twelve months of war. There were other difficulties. 'We are doing all we possibly can to ensure that *The Strand Magazine* reaches you punctually each month, but necessarily there may be a delay owing to the dislocation of transport caused by air raids.'

In January 1941 the magazine was cut back to 72 pages again, with 20 pages of advertising. The price was raised to one-and-threepence. To make the most of the compressed editorial space a smaller type was used, enabling more lines to be got into a page. Illustrations were limited. Short stories were shorter, conditions that suited the work of Will Scott, whose precise craftsmanship was as admirable as O. Henry's.

Short stories provided relief from the war theme. Articles exploited it. The individual reader no longer counted. The magazine was edited for groups, whose organised idleness in wartime encouraged the reading habit. *Heroes of Coastal Command, Squadron Badges of the R.A.F., Feeding the Forces, Radio in War*: the Services were only too ready to co-operate with photographs, facilities, and information. *Esprit de corps* did the rest, so far as *The Strand* was concerned. If its circulation did not greatly benefit, it was held at a still tolerable level.

2

As the year advanced towards autumn the whole newspaper and periodical publishing industry felt the strain of increased paper prices. No new periodicals were permitted. Drastic decision-making was imminent in the Newnes firm. Twenty of its publications were suspended or merged, some of them profitable, so that the paper supplies should be available for others, *The Strand* among them.

That it too did not go to the sacrifice was in some degree an act of pious regard for its former prestige and for the memory of Sir George Newnes. From the economic standpoint, its viability seemed to be just about exhausted. As a result of the latest paper crisis its circulation was guaranteed at 95,000. It was no longer an important property in the commercial sense.

September 1941 saw the end of the old familiar format. No one took it as an omen that the name of the writer of the last short story in that climacteric issue was S. H. Small. By the next month, the magazine was down to pocket-size. Empurpled with rage at the change, Reeves Shaw terminated his long connection with Newnes, and departed to edit a humorous weekly for the Forces.

The declension was abrupt but not startling. Small magazines were not less logical than tabloid newspapers. Nor was there anything radically new in the 'pocket' concept. Based on the notion of giving 'permanent booklet form' to articles condensed from leading magazines, the *Reader's Digest* had established it as a successful formula, one of the most successful in publishing history. That few of its imitators, either in the United States or the United Kingdom, had survived was not necessarily a criticism of the size. *The Countryman*, the book-like quarterly published from an Oxfordshire manor house, handsomely endorsed its popularity on both sides of the Atlantic. Certain old *Strand* advertisers did not find it convenient to adapt their layouts and blocks to the new requirements. The difficulty never became a serious risk in making the transition.

3

Experimenting with the first six or eight issues in the new style, R. J. Minney, who had made a success of *Everybody's Weekly*, worked hard to discover a satisfactory programme for what in effect was a brand-new magazine. He resurrected some of the old colour blocks of Churchill's pictures used in *The Strand* in 1921, and printed on facing pages, also in colour, examples of Hitler's artistic efforts. There was no mistaking which was the superior amateur talent. He persuaded Shaw and Wells to return to a topic that they had jointly discussed in *The Strand* years before: *Do You Believe In A Future Life?* The question was 'insistent today amid the stress and sorrow of war'. Shaw reckoned it 'better to face death than eternity'. Wells could see nothing in the conscious individual life 'worth carrying over and no means of carrying it over'. Conscious life, he pointed out, is dependent on the supply of aerated blood to the brain. 'When that stops, we stop.'

There were other opinions. For J. B. Priestley it was 'a very complicated problem, and both the atheists who say No and the orthodox religious who say Yes are over-simplifying it'. The Dean of St Paul's, the Very Rev. W. R. Matthews, wrote that, without doing violence to his intelligence, he could accept 'the assurance of Revelation that death has been overcome and eternal life is open to all'.

By then it was becoming manifest that the change from big to little had been too much for the loyalty of many old readers, who were not being replaced in sufficient numbers to arrest the circulation decline. It fell to 80,000, a crisis stage at which I was asked to apply my then somewhat dormant editorial instincts to a more immediately pressing problem of survival.

I had to accept the fact that in the Second World War, I was middle-aged, a life pensioner from the old war, and in the military sense no good. I had great difficulty in being considered for any sort of war service, though my name had been on the National Register from the beginning. After many abortive interviews, vexing delays, and some string-pulling in which Sir Walter (later Lord) Monckton was helpful, I secured a post in the home news censorship department of the Ministry of Information. From there I was transferred to the B.B.C. to write, edit, and help to produce overseas editions of Radio Newsreel, work that I continued to do after taking over the editorship of *The Strand Magazine*.

4

The reduction in the size and, in consequence, of the sales of the magazine, meant a reduced editorial budget. It was never defined in figures. No one from on high told me: You cannot spend more than so much in future on stories, articles, illustrations, and what else. When the time came, I was as free to recommend paying Winston Churchill the thousand pounds he asked for the right to reproduce his paintings as I was to offer forty guineas for a story or twenty for an article.

It was none the less clear that rates of payment would have to be pruned, to the dismay of some writers and artists who fancied that by retaining its famous title the magazine was still a wealth-producing organism, able to buy the best and pay accordingly. In some cases that unrealistic notion led to halved fees and disappointment. I remember Kingsley Martin, then editor of the *New Statesman*, insisting that Newnes 'must be making a load of money' out of *The Strand* at one-and-threepence.

The truth was that the magazine had shown no spectacular profit since the early '30s, although outside the boardroom its status remained undimmed. That its title was still gilded with renown was shown by the invitations to public functions addressed to the editor and by the allocation to him of a special place in the table plans. Foreign embassies continued to be deferential.

My job of trying to restore the magazine's fortunes in the new circumstances was made more agreeable by the propinquity of an old friend in the Newnes organisation, Reginald Arkell, who edited another magazine along the corridor and who was well known to the gardening public as the poet of *Green Fingers* and, later, as the author of a best-selling novel called *Old Herbaceous*. He had written the stage version of *1066 And All That*, and a number of other things for the theatre, where, as a son of the Cotswolds, he seemed to be not uncomfortably out of his element. He had something of the appearance and style of a young Will Rogers; the reflective smile, the dependable good sense.

We had known each other for twenty years. We both came from similar country stock. We had the same point of view about many matters, including the perverse temper of Reeves Shaw, for whom Arkell's talents and success were apt to be one of the flash-points of his terrible explosions of jealousy. Arkell's wall-eyed smile was a charm against the worst that could befall.

He himself was beset by a daemon that inhibited any mention in his company of age and death. He did not give his years in *Who's Who* and always avoided any risk of the subject coming up in conversation. He never attended funerals or memorial services. He also had a deep abiding fear of being out of a job. That misfortune occurred to him in the early '30s when a weekly paper that he was editing for the Amalgamated Press collapsed under him. In spite of his artfully contrived moves to meet such an event, his services were not retained.

For a year he went about in a state of apprehension. When I printed some verses by him in the *Daily Mail*, he responded as if I were a benefactor instead of a merely appreciative literary editor. He never ceased to be grateful, reminding me of it years after. Evidently his sojourn in the wilderness was a disturbing experience. Yet he was more gifted than most men who lose jobs in journalism or, for that matter, who get them. He recovered his poise, combined new editorial labours with writing novels that interested the film companies, and acquired a modest fortune.

His mental agility made him a delightful office colleague. I asked him if he had an idea for filling a suddenly vacant double-spread (two facing pages) in the make-up. In half an hour he laid on my desk some lines which he called *Farandole*, composed for the emergency, suggesting that they should be illustrated by Barribal, a brilliant colourist.

Edgar Wallace (seated), who wrote many stories for *The Strand*,
discussing his marathon writing feat described on page 130.

The above picture was used to illustrate the controversial article written by Conan Doyle for the Christmas 1921 issue of *The Strand Magazine*. He claimed that fairies had been photographed, as shown.

New tempo: two pictures from the last issue of *The Strand Magazine*, March 1950.

He was a page at old Versailles. A pretty boy with roguish eye; I seem to see him yet. He stood beside the royal throne; he loved his queen and her alone, his Marie Antoinette.

If all the tales they tell are true, she loved his roguish eyes of blue, and to that cabinet he often came when none could see, though he was just a page, and she was Marie Antoinette.

Alas, too soon sweet moments fly. They sent him far from old Versailles; but he did not forget those golden days, when he had been the chosen champion of a queen, his Marie Antoinette.

I told this story to a boy—bell-hop at our own Savoy—this tale of Marie Antoinette; of how the Queen, left all alone, sat sadly on her royal throne, to dream in vain regret.

The youngster merely turned his head towards the lift; then smiled and said: 'You ain't seen nothin' yet!'

He was a sagacious and witty man whose miniaturist's focus on life did not prejudice the broad, amused compassion with which he regarded the rest of us.

5

Close to our mould and style was the American magazine called *Coronet*, which had achieved a large sale as 'a book-size magazine of popular culture'. Later in the war, its editor, Bernard Geis, came to London. From him I learnt that he was watching *The Strand* with an equally acquisitive eye.

As the war months went by we bought stories and articles freely from American sources, the home supply of talent running exceedingly low. Formerly, an average of four thousand unsolicited stories a year passed through *The Strand Magazine* office. The flow was continuous, if of little value. In the 1940s it fell away almost to zero. Even the more yearning aspirants were not trying any more.

The short story problem remained with us. Readers demanded 'names' that were no longer available at our prices, if at all. 'Why not Somerset Maugham?' I was asked by Sir Frank Newnes, son of the founder, who had a figurehead position in the business, with no influence but that of a kindly nature. He also wondered why not Sherlock Holmes all over again. It had not occurred to him that the stories would be far too long for our 96 pages.

It was not only a question of finance. Certain writers of fiction did not care for the idea of a dwarf *Strand*. One of them was P. G. Wodehouse, of whose professional career the magazine had long been a mainstay. He now wrote disparagingly of it to a friend. Occasionally readers asked why we had no more stories from him. I was glad not to have to make that editorial decision, for I was never able to read Wodehouse's stories or to understand the ecstasy they roused in others. Their appeal to pre-war readers of *The Strand* was apparently irresistible. I could only see it as a phenomenon of extended immaturity, an effect of the more enclosed forms of English education. Wodehouse was an oddity in being an Edwardian before that fleeting epoch and in remaining one ever after.

6

The ratio of short stories to articles was reversed. We stamped the magazine with its own note of authority, muted but informed. *Why should London rule?* we demanded, seeing that the country was being efficiently run by eleven regional commissioners, paving the way to the postwar decentralisation that many thought desirable. Why not a return to self-government for provincial England, with Northumbria, Mercia, Wessex, and East Anglia preserving and accentuating local life and character?

Dean Inge pondered England's future in another light. 'Organised Labour will abuse power as much as the oligarchs did in the eighteenth century and the plutocrats did in the nineteenth. Power is always abused.' He rejected Spengler's theory that nations grow old and die like individuals. 'Biologically, the theory lacks support.' Historically it was true that nations have decayed, but they did not die a natural death. For example, China and Egypt: 'they have had very long lives.' For the time being, there was a dearth of first-class ability, 'but a lot of good work is being done, except perhaps in the fine arts'.

Incredibly, it now seems, Professor Denis Brogan was writing in *The Strand* on: *If the British Empire Disappeared.* Weighing up the possibility as a political scientist, he could insist that 'not until an obvious alternative is in sight will it be prudent or even liberal to assume that the days of the British Empire are numbered or that this is a matter for naïve rejoicing'. Today, a little more than two decades later, the disappearance of the greatest of all empires has become one of history's absolutes.

Other experts of high standing (e.g., Julian Huxley, Liddell Hart, Professor Andrade) answered readers' questions on subjects from astronomy to zoology in *One-Man Brains Trust*, a compelling regular feature that, in adding to the stock of possibly superfluous information, provided good reading by the way. *Perplexities*, borrowed from the old *Strand*, was converted into *Self-Quiz Department*, challenging the mental stagnation of wartime. *Auto-Obituaries* produced a series of intriguing self-evaluations that led to readers making music in the editor's ear by asking for more.

Negley Farson, the vivid, muscular, blue-eyed author of *Way of a Transgressor*, who, at his best, was one of the most attractive of men, imagined himself dying 'on a tropic isle in a fit of convulsive laughter lasting for days, after sitting through the farce of peace and disarmament conferences and reading what the Intellectuals have to say in our political weeklies'. In fact, when his time came eighteen years later, he was listening to a B.B.C. news bulletin, which suggests that the ironic gods had at least taken note of his prognostic exercise.

James Bridie, the dramatist, who in private life was O. H. Mavor, M.D., put the date of his demise as April 1, 1955; the scene of it, 'a box at the Haymarket'; the cause, coronary thrombosis. 'It is true,' he wrote in *The Strand*, 'that he lived by his wits but his living seemed to be a by-product of his wits rather than their main activity.' His prediction that he would leave a wife and two children was all too soon falsified. He lost one of his sons in a burning tank on the battlefield. The shock was thought to have contributed to his own end, which came in 1951.

I spent an afternoon with him and his wife at their house at Drymen in the Campsie Hills, and found it an invigorating experience to talk to one of Scotland's first-rate characters.

After that, I met him from time to time in London, never without being glad of the opportunity to do so. He was a man of excellent humour.

'The name of H. G. Wells, who died yesterday afternoon of heart failure in the Paddington Infirmary at the age of 97, will have few associations with the younger generation,' and one can catch the note of Puckish exuberance as he went on to write that he was 'one of the most prolific literary "hacks" of that time'.

Looking back on his life's labours, Wells likened them to those of a reef-building coral polyp. 'Scarcely anything remains of him now, and yet, without him and his like, the reef of common ideas on which our civilisation stands today could never have arisen.' His epitaph perhaps consists of the six hundred entries under his name in the catalogue of the British Museum reading room. Some of the best of his early work appeared in *The Strand*.

I met him more than once. He was not cordial on casual acquaintance. He would fix you with the analytical eye that had pored over natural history specimens in his days as a biological student. Not a profound thinker, and a writer who seldom rose above the facility of the journalist, he was the seer and prophet of the legatees of the Education Act of 1870; an emancipating force in his prime. Later, it seemed that in his shrill impeachments he showed a want of dignity and of the Stoic temper. But his name had a tocsin ring through the formative years of a generation, and when the news of his death was given out over the radio on August 13, 1946, the effect was as of the end of an epoch, where in truth it was no more than the passing of an exhausted and disgruntled old man. The next day, prompted by me, the *Daily Express* reprinted the obituary notice that he wrote for *The Strand* four years before.

7

General Wavell, at his Middle East headquarters, read an article in *The Strand* on military genius: author, Captain Liddell Hart. 'The article set me reflecting on the art of generalship,' Wavell wrote to *The Times*, which published two articles giving his considered views on that primary topic of the day. Reading the articles, I decided that it would be good policy to reprint them in the magazine that had provided their inspiration. I obtained permission to make cuts that would lighten the load on our pages.

Wavell's assessments made instructive reading that brought us letters from the Royal Navy as well as from the Army. Alexander the Great was 'a brilliant meteor' in the military firmament, placed 'below the steadier stars'. Belisarius was 'a peculiar favourite' of his. Hannibal, Scipio, and Julius Caesar were lower in his rating. Frederick the Great was 'a smash-and-grab Prussian', who merited a high place for his policy of 'attack at all costs'. Cromwell was not deserving of comparable elevation.

Wavell thought that Lawrence of Arabia's field of action and exploits were on 'too small a scale, however great his natural capacity and however deep his study of war'. He also struck out the names of three gifted American Civil War generals—Sherman, Forrest and Stonewall Jackson. 'They were never in supreme command and never had to bear the final strain of responsibility.'

He counted Marlborough 'the greatest commander produced by the British race'. He regarded Napoleon as 'a supreme strategist but an indifferent tactician'. Wellington was a master of defence, 'possibly the soundest of all the great generals'. Neither Foch nor Ludendorff was in the front rank. He summed up: Marlborough and Belisarius first; then Wellington and Frederick the Great; and finally Lee and Napoleon.

Shortly afterwards, the *World's Press News* saluted us with the announcement: '*The Strand Magazine* has adopted the modern format with striking success.' The commendation was earned in the largest measure by A. E. Baker, a *Strand* assistant editor of long experience, and Gordon Stapley, director of the Carlton Studio, as advisory consultant on the art side. Despite the often daunting wartime complications of producing a magazine that was edited in London and printed in Buckinghamshire, Baker's unfaltering hand ensured that there was no breakdown of the monthly routine during the war years.

Stapley's highly contemporary flair saw to it that any temptation to slip back into the old grooves was firmly resisted.

Nor can certain freelance writers be overlooked in a fair assessment of services rendered at that time of trouble. Without them the magazine would have been a less meritorious production, particularly in respect of the articles of topical interest to which the newspapers could no longer give adequate space. Gordon Beckles, George Edinger, William Holt, Martin Chisholm, David Arkell, Gordon Glover, among others, did useful work in the often difficult circumstances of those war years.

Gordon Beckles, who also used two pseudonyms, was the doyen of the group, a familiar and well-liked figure in Fleet Street. The son of Beckles Willson, an English-born Canadian who worked with the young Alfred Harmsworth on the *Daily Mail*, he looked as if his personality and style had been devised for him by Max Beerbohm. Tall and upstanding, with a size-too-small black felt hat resting on top of his head, a well-rolled umbrella pendant from his left wrist, he strolled through wartime London with the air of a clubman of Thackeray's day disdaining the convulsions of history. He had a delightful chuckling humour that was often sharpened into mordant wit. He was charming to know. He did good things for *The Strand*, often in conditions of personal stress, for he was a silently suffering asthmatic. His articles were informative and entertaining annotations of the period.

It was due to so much unstinted co-operation that a day came, in 1943, when a letter was placed on my desk from the chairman of the Newnes board. 'We are very pleased with your work for *The Strand*.' With it there was a generous cheque. We had halted the circulation drift. The figure was rising again, past the 100,000 mark.

SEVENTEEN

The Editor's Portrait Gallery

I

American soldiers called at the office to ask our help in identi-
fying the Baker Street address of Sherlock Holmes. There were
requests for his autograph, of which it was assumed we
had specimens. A United States airman wanted an introduction
to Conan Doyle, dead twelve years.

Those contacts led to American servicemen being invited
to write their impressions of England for *The Strand*. The
offer was made through their army newspaper, *Stars & Stripes*.
It brought us a considerable pile of manuscripts, from which
it appeared that a strong Teutonic influence had formed American calligraphy. To Private W. Hogan it was apparent that 'the
English are fighting for a lot of things. Not to get them, but
to preserve them'. Sergeant M. E. Healey regarded the Royal
Air Force 'with respect and admiration'. As for English people,
'they are too damned polite—they even thank you when you
take something from them'.

Corporal W. L. Blaylock was amazed by the Englishman's
gift for improvisation. 'I met a chap who had a tiny shop in his
backyard. For tools he had a couple of beat-up old wrenches
(spanners), a drill press ingeniously made out of a pile of junk,
and a small lathe of ancient vintage. He was building parts on
contract for national defence and, so help me, you couldn't
tell but what the finished article hadn't been manufactured
in a Chrysler or a General Motors factory.' On the subject of
harmony between the two nations, Private Bruce Fessenden
insisted that 'there's no need to wait till the war is over. We
damned well understand each other right now'.

If the sentiments were unexceptional, the voices were those
of men who were free to speak their minds. They had crossed

a wide ocean to uphold that right. There were no signs of illiteracy. The level of competent, unaffected self-expression was probably higher than in the rank and file of our army. One had a sense of being in touch with an exceedingly robust democracy.

2

Hitler's addiction to astrology incited the inquiry: *Do The Stars Foretell*? In spite of paper shortages, space was still found for the astrology columns. *The Strand* examined the credentials of the leading practitioners. Foremost was R. H. Naylor, who had a large following in the *Sunday Express*. Not long before the war I walked up Kingsway with John Gordon, then editor of that newspaper. A lightly built, oval-faced man came towards us. 'You're looking worried, Naylor,' Gordon said, having introduced us. 'What's the trouble?' The prophet of fate and destiny bit hard on his pipe stem before replying in a Northern accent: 'It's this bloody alimony that gets me down.'

We sent the astrology article in proof to the Astronomer Royal, Sir Harold Spencer Jones, F.R.S., asking for his comments. He wrote urging that 'a strong stand' should be made against the cult. 'From various instances brought to my notice, I know that it is productive of suffering and unhappiness.' He asserted that there is no logical or scientific justification for astrology as a professional practice.

Meeting him, I found that his stern objective view was tinged by a private prejudice. He constantly received letters from persons who believed that it was part of the Astronomer Royal's duties to cast horoscopes. 'What fools these mortals be,' I quoted, with no obvious satisfaction to him.

Television, shut down from the outbreak of war, was bound to reassert itself on a wider scale when circumstances permitted. The B.B.C.'s experimental programmes broadcast from Alexandra Palace, London, N., had shown that, technically, England was well out in front as the originator of the world's first regular television service. Now, in the middle of the war, the chairman of the governors of the B.B.C. was promising 'majority viewing in twenty years'.

The Strand contrasted that prospect with what had so far been accomplished. B.B.C. television had been confined to a sixty-mile radius from Alexandra Palace, London, N., serving the metropolis and the home counties only. There were complaints from radio listeners in the North that their licence fees were subsidising viewing in the South. About 20,000 sets had been in regular use, with a conservatively estimated viewing audience of 50,000. At the 1939 Radio Olympia orders for sets at £30 each increased twenty-fold.

There had been 18 staff producers on the payroll at Alexandra Palace, where B.B.C. television operated. Their production budgets ranged between £150 and £500. Daily programmes consisted mainly of mannequin parades, cookery demonstrations, physical exercises, newsreels, film cartoons, and a miscellany feature called Picture Parade, compèred by Leslie Mitchell and Joan Gilbert. Theatre chains would not allow their plays to be televised. They banned actors and actresses from working for television.

A lanky, long-haired, soft-voiced Scot named John Logie Baird was interviewed at his Sydenham Hill studio. He told *The Strand* that he had twenty patents covering colour television and stereoscopic vision. 'Mr Baird states that he is prepared to produce a set embodying all these features, immediately peace is declared, for £15.'

George Orwell's face showed incredulity when I told him that the best-known comic picture-postcard artist, Donald McGill, had called on me at *The Strand* office. Orwell had written about his work in *Horizon*, mentioning that he had been unable to trace McGill, a name that he consequently believed to be that of a syndicate of artists. Hitherto, McGill's identity was a secret. Now he wanted reassurance from me that his work was not 'smutty', not so suggestively harmful as some people thought. He was a man of education who remarked, as an endorsement of his respectability, that at the old boys' dinner of his public school he was 'always put next to the Bishop of Wakefield'.

He had the style of a naval commander and showed himself to be widely read. His 'dirty' postcards, which sold by tens of millions at the seaside every summer, had enabled him to gather round him a fine library in his Surrey home.

Many of those wartime issues of *The Strand* were made-up to the sound of howling sirens and crashing bombs, with the interruptions of retreat into the corridors; rarely into the shelters below. When the possibility of dislocation seemed imminent, we moved the office to Ballinger Grange, near Great Missenden, which gave us easier access to the printers, Hazell, Watson & Viney, at Aylesbury. By the end of three weeks I was writing in my diary: 'This rural life is not a success editorially. We cannot run the magazine by telephone.' A peculiar difficulty was the briefing of writers and artists, particularly the passing of 'roughs' for illustrations. We went back to Southampton Street, our return coinciding with the first flying bomb attacks on London. In Aldwych, three hundred yards away, one killed 44 persons. Then came the rockets.

3

A new salvage drive settled the fate of the array of heavily-mounted photographs of noted *Strand* story writers that were part of the office heritage from Greenhough Smith's time: Rider Haggard, Conan Doyle, Rudyard Kipling, W. W. Jacobs, A. E. W. Mason, H. G. Wells, William le Queux, P. G. Wodehouse, W. J. Locke, 'Sapper', Stacy Aumonier, Hugh Walpole, and others. There was only one beard among them.

The most striking face was Aumonier's, darkly aquiline, his forelock curving across his brow, under which were set deep piercing eyes. He always wore a black stock and looked unidentifiably professional. He came from a family of Spitalfields silversmiths and his sense of craftsmanship was delicate and sincere. There was general critical agreement that his death at 41 put an end to a fine improving talent: see, for example, his short stories collected in *Three Bars Interval*.

Kipling's first name was Joseph, revealed when he became a Freemason. The London *Academy*, I discovered, had some fun with it in verse:

I went into a library to get a book to read,
The man behind the counter asked: 'What is it, sir, you need?'
'I want,' I said, 'the latest thing that Joseph Kipling's done.'

'Go on,' he said, 'you're having me. Joe Kip? There isn't one!'
O, it's Brother Joe, and Joseph, when insignias are out,
And knives and forks are busy, and the bottle goes about.
It's 'Brother Joe from India' where'er the Masons throng,
But it's Rudyard Kipling only when he writes a blooming song.

Both Kipling and Conan Doyle experienced down-phases at the turn of the century. 'The Kipling of a few years ago, rushing about from editor to editor, from publisher to publisher, with a dressing-case full of wonderful Indian tales was sublime, whereas the affluent and rather cocky Kipling of today, the Kipling of *The Day's Work*, of "the white man's burden", and *Stalky & Co.*, is—well, his wretched fizzling out is painful and pathetic.'[1] A Yale professor was reported as saying: 'Mr Kipling's great mistake was that he did not die of pneumonia when he was ill in New York seven or eight years ago.'[2]

Kipling was on his guard against fickle popularity. He wrote to a friend after being lionised at a reception at Rutland Gate, London: 'Unless it happened that I was the fashion for the moment, they'd let me die of want on your doorstep and so they would.'

Conan Doyle had been cited in the same critical context as 'a striking example of the pitiful uncertainty of literary success. Somehow, the edge of the appetite for his work has been dulled, and we wonder rather curiously as we recall the ardour, the zest, the enthusiasm with which we awaited each new problem for Sherlock Holmes to solve'.

The suggestion that Doyle had reached his literary dotage was refuted when in 1903 Holmes reappeared in *The Strand Magazine* which had a mass of readers for whom the old magic was still potent. Connoisseurs of the game preferred the earlier Holmes stories, which they considered unmatched by any that came after. Monsignor Knox wrote: 'I reverence the old stories of the Holmes cycle, I reverence them as old classics, models on which all later work in the same field has been based.' To him, Conan Doyle's later Holmes stories were, 'to put criticism at its mildest, unworthy of his fame'.[3]

[1] *The Bookman* (U.S.A.), 1900.
[2] *Ibid*, 1906.
[3] R. A. Knox: *Literary Distractions* (Sheed & Ward, 1958).

William Tufnell le Queux (1864–1927) was one of the story-tellers who had no genius, no wit and little humour, and who yet drew you into the mainstream of his narrative with his first three sentences and held you there willingly breasting the tide of conspiracy, killing, loving and treasure-hunting, until the climax came, resounding and complete. He was a Londoner who in a varied life was foreign editor of *The Globe*, a *Daily Mail* war correspondent in the Balkans, and consul for the Republic of San Marino. For some years he lived at Leghorn, a neighbour and friend of Mascagni, composer of *Cavalleria Rusticana*.

Le Queux's fiction province was the secret service. He claimed to have 'special knowledge' of its ramifications in Central Europe and the Middle East, and to have been consulted 'on such matters' by the Government. When he caused the supremely fascinating heroine of his novel *Zoraida* to be married prosaically at St Paul's, Knightsbridge, a critic considered it 'the greatest outrage on the romantic feeling that we ever remember to have had practised on us'.

In 1910, he published an invasion novel in which a Prussian army captured London and hanged prominent British citizens in front of Dorchester House, Park Lane. The general thesis of the novel, which ran into fourteen editions, was seriously discussed by the reviewers.

During the war that he had fictionally forecast, he came unpleasantly close to bankruptcy as a result of a rash publishing venture. He wrote a book, *Can We Win?* and published it at his own expense, buying the paper and giving an optimistically large print order. The book was censored and had to be withdrawn. Floundering in shallow financial water, he wrote to Lord Northcliffe: 'Can you save me?' Northcliffe an exceptionally generous man, sent him a cheque with the message: 'I never lend money, but I am glad to give help when and where I think it is needed.'

His style was as racy as Edgar Wallace's, with a tincture of taste that Wallace did not have. He collected medieval manuscripts and monastic seals, on which he became an authority. He was skilled in plot construction and in unfolding events with the directness and simplicity that makes the born story-teller independent of the critics. Most of the writers in Greenhough Smith's private pantheon qualified for that immunity.

W. J. Locke's face suggested precision of thought and habit. He was a mathematics honours man at Cambridge and later taught that subject in Northern schools. It was not an experience that he enjoyed. He wrote of it as 'school slavery, teaching children the most useless, the most disastrous, the most soul-cramping branch of knowledge'. More to his liking was the post of senior French master at the Oxford Military College, Temple Cowley. Subsequently he was at Clifton College, Bristol, and Trinity College, Glenalmond, teaching modern languages. For France, he had an inalienable affection.

He had studied architecture with sufficient thoroughness as a layman to qualify for the post of secretary to the Royal Institute of British Architects, which he held for ten years. Having written two successful novels, *The Morals of Marcus Ordeyne* and *The Beloved Vagabond*, he felt secure enough to take up the professional writing life.

That his fastidious nature found satisfaction in the picaresque was one of the minor enigmas of the human heart. Was Locke trying to shake the early mathematical disciplines out of his head or reacting from the class restraints of which he was in many respects the precise embodiment? *The Beloved Vagabond* was not a novel so much as the history of a temperament. Its chief figure, Paragot, the son of a Gascon father and an Irish mother, became in his creator's hands a bowdlerised Villon, symbol of a freedom of personality that Locke envied while also enjoying the comfort of knowing that it was beyond his attainment. In his stories there was an indefinable charm compounded of the romantic, the Quixotic, and the ironic. Combined with his sincerity and sympathy, and his unobtrusive respect for ideals, it gained him the loyalty of a large magazine public. As was said of another writer for *The Strand*, 'he could be read without interference with the digestive organs'.

So we parted for ever with those photographs of the great ones of *The Strand* past, and asked readers in a following issue: 'What sort of short stories do you prefer? There is a fashion, unlikely to be less ephemeral than any other, for stories that are undeniably short but which are not so much stories as incidents got up to look like stories. No doubt the old romantic-style story, with its hackneyed hero or cad, and the indispensable girl, has died the death. At least this tear may be dropped—it did cheer you up rather than cast you down. Ought we to stand for a more robust type of short story, or do you prefer the prevailing masquerade of the boneless wonder in short story writing?'

Behind our somewhat plaintive appeal was a hope that it would stimulate writers capable of combining robust narrative with the brevity suited to our wartime condition. We received, in response, requests for stories by Maugham, Mason, and Wodehouse; and a threat from a reader to abandon us if we published another Wodehouse story. Literary agents sent us large envelopes crammed with stuff they had obviously not bothered to read, most of it of the anaemic, spun-out-incident kind.

4

Harold Laski, the professorial Socialist with the extraordinary speaking manner, joined in our series, *What They Did for England*, with a rousing review of Churchill's character and career, proclaiming that his virtues were as monumental as his weaknesses. 'The real Churchill is imperialist, paternalist, in favour of a strong government which shelters the weak from the blasts of life. He would hate a world which found no room for the romantic Empire-builder. Will he end his career in a blaze of glory or, like the Duke of Wellington after Waterloo, seem like some splendid but obsolete survival of a vanished epoch?'

Meeting General de Gaulle fortuitously and alone left me with so favourable an impression of him as a man that I commissioned an article about him as the likeliest Frenchman to lead his nation back to recovery. I was sure that there were qualities in him that counted for greatness equal to Churchill's. Churchill had reached his full stature in war. De Gaulle would realise his destiny in peace. We decided that 'it is very unlikely that his career will end with the liberation of France. ... His will undoubtedly be the most eloquent and authoritative French voice'. It was no paean of praise. 'On many minds he produces an impression of an obstinate, narrow, ambitious seeker after power.' There was mention of his sardonic, choleric temper, and embarrassing bluntness. Having had a good look at him at unexpectedly close range, I was sure that he had attractive complementary characteristics.

On the subject of leadership, we asked Liddell Hart to comment on the position of the junior officers in the Second World War, remembering that it was in their ranks in the First World War that the nation suffered some of its most grievous losses. He wrote that 'the junior leaders have always borne the brunt of war, and do so still; but they have now become the most important mental factor in determining the issue. That', he emphasised, 'should be remembered when peace comes.'

Leaders with a less inspiring mission were considered in *The Big Five of Midnight Music*. They were the men who brandished the 'stick' at the Café de Paris, the Embassy Club, the Mayfair, the Savoy, and in the B.B.C. studios: Debroy Somers, who looked like an Army bandmaster and was the son of one; Ambrose, 'aristocrat of the dance band world', Geraldo, 'soigné spider in a spangled web', Roy, 'small, twinkle-eyed, tense, and working like the devil', Payne, the stiff-backed maestro of the original B.B.C. dance orchestra. Other names spring from the page, stirring flocks of febrile echoes from the wartime past: Ternant, Loss, Hall, Parry, Lipton.

No less loudly prominent in 'show business' then were the theatre organists, a new race of entertainers whom we pictured as wizards playing with their 'giant boxes of tricks', their repertoires full of brazen contrasts: the *1812 Overture* and *Swanee River*, *Ave Maria* and *The Wedding of the Painted Doll*. Wurlitzer, Christie and Compton organs ministered to the overheated emotions of the period. Their mighty chords surged and swelled in The Tower Ballroom, Blackpool (Reginald Dixon); the Forum, Southampton (Reginald Porter-Brown); the Regal, Beckenham (Reginald New); Brighton Gaumont (Felton Rapley); the Capitol, Aberdeen (Harold Coombes); the Empire, Leicester Square (Sandy Macpherson).

We, too, were capable of sounding notes of deep sonority, suggesting, for example, 'better ways of commemorating our war dead than by parades, ceremonial unveilings, and uninspiring lumps of stone'. Old war memorials were photographed and presented as examples of civic bad taste. 'Why not rededicate the Cenotaph in Whitehall as the national symbol and let local memorials take a more constructive form—playing fields, hospital wings, clinics, parks, gardens?'

'What gives you hope in times like these?' was a question we put to a leading physiologist, Professor V. H. Mottram. He found reassurance, he said, in those moments of illumination that some have of hints of the truth behind the phenomenon of life. 'Man's next conquests lie in the realm of the spirit. There will be found oceans, trackless, uncharted, perhaps dangerous. Modern man must launch out on that voyage of exploration if he is to find his soul.'

From 1944 on we were looking with sober confidence to a future that was still shadowed but never in doubt. 'What postwar reform would you most like to see?' was a question that went out to several prominent persons. Perhaps it was a symptom of national tiredness that the answers were prosaic. An admiral wanted 'adequate playing fields for all school children', a Conservative member of Parliament put commercial radio first on his list of priorities, a hospital chairman proposed a return to penny postage. A music critic urged the nationalisation of the legal profession.

A keener sense of urgency was shown by wartime refugees in Britain, asked what ideas they would want to take home with them when the hour of liberation came. An Amsterdam housewife, Mevrouw Betsy Kiek, hoped to be able to transplant in Holland the Citizens' Advice Bureau, an English institution that she thought socially valuable. Dr Ivo Duchacek, of Brno, Czechoslovakia, would have liked his countrymen to adopt the English code of the unwritten agreement in business. 'You rely on the honesty of the other fellow. That will definitely stay in my mind when I go back.' Madame Leonine Wowalska, a Warsaw housewife, wrote: 'I think of England and say: that is a right country, a fair country. You listen to everyone to put his case. Your laws are above Party. I think it is marvellous that the judge is so high standing.' From Baard Krogvig, publisher, of Oslo, came the reply: 'I get an evening newspaper which is supposed to be Conservative and there I read a Socialist article! Your tolerance and your free expression of all points of view is good. This is what I will take back with me to Norway.'

As a corrective of national self-esteem, it seemed desirable to print the findings of an inquiry on Anglo-American relations carried out among 500 New York City school children by the education editor of the *New York Times*. It showed that the seeds of misunderstanding between the two nations were sprouting strongly among the new generation of Americans. The general tone indicated mistrust and dislike. 'Fully one-third answered "no" to the question: Should England and America work closely together after the war?'

EIGHTEEN

Last Editor, Last Issue

I

Driving up to town from Chartwell, Westerham, in the late summer of 1945, after spending most of an afternoon in Winston Churchill's garden studio, looking at the large number of his paintings that covered the walls and stood stacked against the skirting, I was seized by the idea of his becoming the nominal, if not practising, editor-in-chief of a reconstituted *Strand Magazine*. Extravagant, absurd, as it now seems, it was not so then. He was back in a wilderness which, if it was not so figless and thorn-ridden as that of his earlier experience, was sufficiently empty of incident to impel his return to journalism. 'I am a member of your profession,' he had reminded me during those bedroom interviews. He sat for ten hectic days in an editor's chair. That was during the General Strike of 1926, when he was in charge of the official newspaper, *The British Gazette*.

The future of *The Strand Magazine* was a recurring preoccupation as the war receded. We had improved the circulation by thirty-five thousand copies. It did not warrant the hope of indefinite continuance. There was no way of deciding how many of the readers were true loyalists and how many the casual captives of wartime leisure. I consulted a wise friend of mine in an opposite camp, John Dunbar, editorial director of Odhams Press.

He believed that *The Strand* could be given back its eminence, that there would be a place for a great new national magazine when paper restrictions were off. He suggested that to launch *The Strand* afresh would cost Newnes £250,000, not an unrealistic figure at the time. We both agreed that the old pre-war uncritical, easy-going conformist line would never serve again, that for survival the magazine could no longer exist as a vehicle of passive entertainment, and mere relaxation. A more positive and creative policy would have to be found for it.

The war was fast receding as a viable topic. Already it was nearly half a decade since young Richard Hillary had walked into my room, his face scars still livid, his hand stump a ghastly souvenir of the air fighting of 1940. Now, crouched in the chair where he had sat was a young artist who survived the desolating experience of captivity in Japanese hands. His name was Ronald Searle. He was still a sick man, his face yellow and drawn, his voice invalidishly low.

He had brought with him a copy of *Exile*, the camp magazine that he and two others, Alan Roberts and Jack Wood, had produced in secret in Changi Prison, Singapore. Its 20,000 words were typed at great risk by a medical orderly. Searle did the illustrations, using clippings of his hair for paint brushes. Dyes for staining laboratory slides supplied his colours. The magazine was an astonishing production, as Lord Louis Mountbatten agreed when he saw it immediately after the prisoners were released in 1945.

We took a last glimpse of the war in the West in an article based on the Nazi guide issued to officers detailed for participation in Operation Sealion, the invasion of England. The numerous elevation drawings, its 50 maps copied from the British Ordnance Survey, and its 400 photographs, were printed on the reverse side of similar plans already carried out in the Netherlands, Luxembourg, and Norway and cancelled in a thick purple ink. The height of every cliff was given, every geological feature noted, every little harbour and cove named. Now, with Germany beaten to the ground, there seemed to have been nothing but madness in all that method.

'Waves of crime follow all wars. There are some worried men at Scotland Yard just now.' One of Fleet Street's best-known crime reporters was scanning the horizon for signs of postwar activity in the underworld. He told our readers that it would probably be reinforced by more men with guns at their hips, as well as new lethal tricks 'in the bag', than in any previous era. War, which brutalises men, also refines the means of brutality.

The 1944 Education Act, which had been in suspense, was extending the school-leaving age as one of its first practical measures. It was an excuse for asking A. L. Rowse, Fellow of All Souls, Oxford, what he considered to be the marks of an educated man. He named tact, taste, critical judgment, and mental economy, among the desired qualities. 'Tact is an underrated virtue, more important than people think.' By Rowse's definition the educated man speaks correct 'standard' English, and 'in manner gives the impression of effortless control, with which go courtesy and ease. He is not taken in by newspapers, propaganda, demagogues, or what else. He compares things, judges between them, and relates them to experience. He chooses the best and rejects the worst'. Rowse put in a strong word, also, for what he called mental resonance— 'receptivity to new experience'.

Religion had lost its grip on the lives of many. Moral standards were sagging. As if to fill a vacuum, there was a pronounced switch of attention to telepathy and kindred phenomena. Professor S. G. Soal, Lecturer in Mathematics, University of London, had been working along the lines of Dr Rhine, at Duke University, U.S.A. In the course of his researches he had an extraordinary spiritualistic experience which, as related by him in *The Strand*, roused the greatest interest. Scores of readers wrote to tell us of mental phenomena that for them represented transcendent experience. Publishing some of the letters, we received scores more that we could not publish for want of space. What seemed remarkable was that perfectly ordinary individuals were reporting events that were like signals from another dimension. My colleague, Reginald Arkell, was moved to write out a telepathic experience of his that resulted in a man being saved from drowning.

2

We had brought *The Strand* through the difficult war years to 1946. Churchill's paintings were published that summer and were a success with readers everywhere. They supplied no assurance of a secure future for a general-interest magazine. The new era would be one of technical emphasis and development. Substantiating that view, Newnes acquired a large interest in Temple Press, Ltd., pioneers in motoring and aviation journalism and publishing. It was a sign of the times in periodical publishing.

A far greater field of specialisation lay open, the promotion of papers for women. It held a vast potential new readership. Abundant colour combined with newspaper techniques would exploit it to the extent of many millions of copies a week. Newnes were resolved to be well forward in that highly competitive branch of the business.

Sentiment, and little else, clinched the sudden decision of the board to cast *The Strand* in a new postwar mould as from October 1946. A scheme of reorganisation was discussed with those involved and carried through without hurt to any. (It was my experience of the Newnes firm, going back to another postwar period, that they were zealous in maintaining the rule of liberal treatment for staff, writers, and artists, laid down by George Newnes in his *Tit-Bits* time.) My successor was an old friend, Macdonald Hastings, who had been brought in to take charge of a proposed new weekly paper to be called *Highway*, never produced. He was the son of Basil Macdonald Hastings, journalist and playwright, whose work for the theatre was marked by perception and wit: e.g. *The New Sin* (1912). His death at 47 was a professional tragedy, apart from the deep distress of it for his family and friends.

The liveliest resource and *brio* were shown in adapting the magazine to the new conditions. An easing of the paper situation allowed a return to 112 pages, as in the beginning. A still more flexible editorial budget permitted the purchase of stories by Somerset Maugham, Georges Simenon, Graham Greene, Edward Ardizzone, Osbert Lancaster, Ronald Searle, and other artists were employed to express the spirit of renaissance that was soon to flower in the Festival of Britain. *The Strand* was a new magazine, but Macdonald Hastings and his team were not above genuflecting to the old. 'Most of us grew up with *The Strand* under our arms. For a middle-aged lifetime this magazine has been part of the English scene.'

They even revived Sherlock Holmes, using the expedient of an apocryphal story, *The Adventure of the First Class Carriage*, written by Ronald Knox, and illustrated by Tom Purvis, 'in loving memory of Sidney Paget'. Some said that Purvis's realisation of Holmes surpassed Paget's.

Nor did they disdain to invoke the old connection with the Court that had been so valuable an asset of the magazine's goodwill in past times. 'By gracious consent of Her Majesty Queen Mary' heralded an illustrated article on the drawing-room at Marlborough House, where the Queen was then resident. More than once, walking along the Mall on my way to the Strand, I had seen her arranging the flowers before the wide open windows of that splendid apartment.

That *The Strand* in its renovated guise was a first-rate contemporary publication could not be disputed. The strength of its new appeal was reflected in the well-filled advertising pages. Circulation remained steady at 125,000. Intensive and ingenious efforts were made on the editorial side to send it soaring again to the old dominant heights. Apart from the problem of defining trends in public taste, economic facts hindered progress. Paper costs had trebled. Distribution charges had risen. There were troublesome labour disputes, involving higher printing bills. Advertising rates could not be raised without a commensurate improvement in the circulation.

Surveying their domain of 53 periodicals, besides other publishing interests, the Newnes board had already decided that there was no case for continuing their once popular literary journal, *John o' London's Weekly*, which for thirty years had catered for the needs of a widely scattered public interested in books. The paper had not earned its keep since the war, making a total loss which approached £50,000 before the closure came. It had been kept alive largely in deference to its value as an educational and cultural medium. Rising costs meant that its reprieve could not be sustained. Reviewed in the same relentless economic light, the position of *The Strand Magazine* was increasingly vulnerable.

3

Listeners to the 6 p.m., 9 p.m., and 10 p.m. Home News bulletins of the B.B.C. on December 13, 1949, heard the following item: '*The Strand Magazine*, pioneer of British illustrated magazines, and for many years the most popular of its kind in the world, is to cease publication with the March issue next year. Announcing this, the publishers, Messrs George Newnes, say the decision has been taken because rising costs and production difficulties have made it impossible to keep up the magazine's traditional standard. *The Strand* began nearly sixty years ago when Sir George Newnes had an idea for a magazine packed with stories and articles with a picture on every page. . . .'

The immediate effect in some quarters was akin to that felt twenty-five years earlier when England went off the gold standard. The news produced the same sense of profound surprise, as of a flaw suddenly appearing in the natural order of things. For those people in particular who had not seen a copy since the days of Sherlock Holmes it was a great shock.

The Times next morning had a third leader, *Farewell To The Strand*. 'The number of monthly magazines that have existed is legion, but only a few have left more than a fleeting memory. Among those few is *The Strand Magazine* . . . As *The Cornhill* in its earlier days caught the spirit of the age of Thackeray and Trollope, *The Strand* was a popular influence of great importance . . . ' *The Times* recalled the association of Kipling and Wells with *The Strand*. ' . . . . As men of letters they were of a higher rank than Doyle, but that is hardly the final criterion for judging such work as the stories in *The Strand*, which depended for their effect more upon plot, character, careful workmanship, and that indefinable storyteller's gift than upon the niceties of literary style . . . '

Regret was the keynote. '*The Strand Magazine* is Dying': a London *Evening Standard* headline; under it a reproduction of the cover of the Christmas Number for 1894. The London *News Chronicle* also sounded the elegiac note. 'No more will the monthly potpourri of humour, drama and life go out from Southampton Street to the bookstalls of the world. No more will exiled Englishmen sigh with nostalgia at the sight of the cover of the famous *Strand*.' It meant the extinction of 'more than a magazine—of a British institution'.

The Economist of December 17, 1949 criticised Newnes's decision to have done with the magazine. 'Its disappearance will be the removal of a landmark as characteristic as those denizens of the same street, Romano's and the Lyceum.' Pointing out that the history of journalism is strewn with the wreckage of good publications that could not make ends meet, *The Economist* insisted that 'the case of *The Strand* is rather different. It is controlled by a publishing house, George Newnes, Ltd., which owns a number of highly successful trade and other papers and which last year reported a net profit of £526,092 on a capital of £1,232,472. It is hard to believe that the resources of a publishing house of this size could not restore a magazine with as much existing goodwill as *The Strand* to its pristine position, redesigned and reorganised to suit contemporary taste'. By way of further reproof, the paper added: 'A publishing house is a business enterprise whose projects must be financially sound, but it is also a trustee of the affections of the reading public in Britain and overseas, and of that public's standards of taste.'

The Economist took no account of increased costs. It also overlooked the vital fact that the overheads of monthly production had become disproportionately higher than those of weekly publication.

Time, the American news weekly, recorded the event as 'the death of a tradition', noting that under Greenhough Smith, '*The Strand* spurred the Edwardian spirit of adventure and empire by travelogues, picture biographies of famous men and foreign correspondence by Winston Churchill'. *Time* referred to the notable scientific articles written for *The Strand* by non-scientists like Grant Allen. '*The Strand* became part of British life, from drawing-room to below stairs, and colonials fondly regarded it as "a bit of London" in their far-off homes.' According to the same source, 'wrote one nostalgic old-timer: "The *Bible*, *Pilgrim's Progress* and *The Strand Magazine* were my first three books." '

In *The Observer*, Ivor Brown proposed that a plaque to *The*

Strand should be put up in Southampton Street.[1] Some commentators suggested that the proliferation of *Penguins* and *Pelicans* had usurped the place of magazines, and that the decline of *The Strand* could be traced back to the high prices paid to authors as a result of 'the exactions and bluffs' of literary agents. Other *post mortem* thoughts were that 'big name' writers had been disinclined to use up in short-story form plots and ideas that could be sold more advantageously to the film companies, and that swifter transport and television were inimical to the magazine habit.

In Fleet Street it was said that the Newnes directors were 'shocked and dismayed' by the public impact of their decision. That was an exaggeration. Their feelings went no deeper than surprise, tinctured by cynicism, when it became obvious that much of the emotion was centred in the title, with its nostalgic associations, rather than in the magazine that bore it. The chairman of Newnes had to suffer the personal reproaches of a prominent man who, it transpired, had no idea that *The Strand* had suffered a change in size nearly ten years before.

The magazine was incurring a serious loss. The circulation had dropped to 95,000 and the secret of stopping the decline was as elusive as the philosopher's stone. There was no warranty for losing more money or for risking the large capital sum required to re-establish the magazine in a form befitting a prestige that survived only in a dwindling number of veteran memories.

Not all in the publishing world accepted the inevitability of doom. There were those who believed that salvation was possible. One of them, Lord Rothermere, chief proprietor of the *Daily Mail*, made a tentative offer to take over the magazine. 'As it did not receive a welcome, I dropped it,' he recalled in a letter to me of November 17, 1964. Other approaches were reported. Newnes could hardly auction the remnants of the magazine's goodwill. Neither could they reasonably have been expected to risk its development elsewhere to the detriment of their own prestige.

[1] The old Newnes building, where *The Strand* was published, remains externally intact.—R.P.

4

Forty-eight hours before the issue for March 1950 was due to go to press, Macdonald Hastings was called down to the Newnes boardroom to be told that the end had come. *The Strand* would cease publication after fifty-nine years. He returned to his desk to write a short valedictory to be printed in the final number.

'The decision to discontinue a magazine with such a past was naturally reached with great reluctance. With paper three times its former price and with all other costs heavily increased, it has become more and more evident that it is not practicable to revert to the traditional character and size of *The Strand Magazine*—a policy deemed essential to maintain its unrivalled prestige throughout the world. Rather, therefore, than mar a glorious record by continuing a policy of expedients, the proprietors, George Newnes, Ltd., have felt compelled to bring its long and distinguished career to a close.'

Having marked the announcement for the printers, he went out into the Strand and bought a mourning band. He wore it on his left sleeve on the last press day in the history of *The Strand Magazine*.

Index